THE STUDENT COMPANION TO
COMMUNITY-ENGAGED LEARNING

THE STUDENT COMPANION TO COMMUNITY-ENGAGED LEARNING

What You Need to Know for Transformative Learning and Real Social Change

David M. Donahue and
Star Plaxton-Moore

Foreword by Tania D. Mitchell
Afterword by Chris Nayve

Routledge
Taylor & Francis Group

NEW YORK AND LONDON

First published 2018 by Stylus Publishing, LLC

First Edition, 2018

Published 2023 by Routledge
605 Third Avenue, New York, NY 10017
4 Park Square, Milton Park, Abingdon, Oxon OX14 4RN

*Routledge is an imprint of the Taylor & Francis Group,
an informa business*

Library of Congress Cataloging-in-Publication Data
Names: Donahue, David M., author. | Plaxton-Moore, Star, author.
Title: The student companion to community-engaged learning : what
you need to know for transformative learning and real social change
/ David M. Donahue and Star Plaxton-Moore ; foreword by Tania
Mitchell ; afterword by Chris Nayve.
Description: First edition. | Sterling, Virginia : Stylus Publishing, 2018. |
Includes bibliographical references and index.
Identifiers: LCCN 2018002638|
ISBN 9781620366486 (cloth : alk. paper) |
ISBN 9781620366493 (pbk. : alk. paper) |
Subjects: LCSH: Service learning--United States. |
Transformative learning--United States. |
Social justice--Study and teaching--United States.
Classification: LCC LC220.5 .D66 2018 |
DDC 372.42/5--dc23
LC record available at https://lccn.loc.gov/2018002638

ISBN 13: 978-1-62036-649-3 (pbk)
ISBN 13: 978-1-62036-648-6 (hbk)
ISBN 13: 978-1-00-344811-2 (ebk)

DOI: 10.4324/9781003448112

This book is dedicated to all the students, faculty, community partners, and McCarthy Center colleagues with whom we have had the privilege to work at USF over the years.

CONTENTS

FOREWORD

I n 1902, 11 years before he became president of the United States, Woodrow Wilson was the president of Princeton University. His insistence that "service is the high law of duty" may be part of the reason why colleges and universities have included civic learning and community engagement as aspects of students' educations for more than a century (Wilson, 1902, p. 97). After all, according to Wilson (1902), "every American university must square its standards by that law or lack its national title" (p. 97). But what does it mean to view service as the "high law of duty"? And, in a time of increasing stratification when the cost of getting an education demands that one prioritize the efficiency of graduating and the study of subjects that best lead to gainful employment, where does service fit?

The answer, I believe, is that service isn't meant to fit; it is meant to be. Service—or more specifically, a full and active engagement with the people, problems, and promises of the community where you live—is what civic education and community engagement experiences prepare people for. Higher education institutions have been trying different strategies to prepare students for this kind of active community membership for some time, and sometimes with more success than others. The work of colleges and universities to provide students with a civic education is aimed with the recognition that we need each and every person to contribute to our democracy in order to truly be a society operating of, for, and by the people. Colleges and universities are uniquely positioned to help students recognize their abilities and opportunities to work for a better society. And although they are uniquely positioned to do this work, they are not always good at it. A research study by Eric Dey and associates (2009) found that of 24,000 students surveyed, only *one-third* felt strongly that their [civic] awareness had *expanded* while in college, that the campus had helped them learn the *skills* needed to effectively change society for the better, or that their *commitment* to change society for the better had grown while in college. (p. viii)

So we have work to do.

Community-engaged learning and the types of learning opportunities that help prepare for full and active engagement with the people, problems, and promises of the community where you live are centered in this text. In chapter 3 the authors ask readers to embrace a set of responsibilities to a community grappling with issues of injustice and marginalization. To accept this task requires the awareness, skills, and commitment that Dey and colleagues saw waning in the students they surveyed.

Community-engaged learning requires a willingness and a desire to get to know people. To see and hear and learn from the individuals who live in the community, who are working to make it better or perhaps struggling to find their place. To listen to their hopes for themselves and their dreams for their community and to come to see yourself as a person who can contribute to that vision. It requires seeing yourself as one of the people working to make it a welcoming, inclusive, and sustainable place that fosters community.

Community-engaged learning requires a recognition of the problems and concerns that make community-building challenging. Communities are places not only of opportunity and celebration but also of trauma and violence. They are spaces where jobs are created and disappear, where homes are built or left to rot, where art beautifies and vandalism scars. In communities, there are people who are healthy and thriving and others who are sick and struggling. Full and active engagement with the problems of a community requires learning about the issues facing people and the systems and structures that create and sustain them. It requires researching what has been done to remedy those concerns and where (and why) those remedies have succeeded or fallen short. It requires organizing with others to identify (or imagine!) new strategies to address those problems so that each member of the community is able to actualize his or her full potential.

Community-engaged learning requires belief in the promises of the community where you live. Communities are not (and are unlikely to be) perfect, but they are beautiful and beloved regardless. It is necessary to believe in and hope for a community where each of its members has everything needed to effectively, authentically, and purposefully participate. Believing in the promise of a community can be difficult, especially when the media, peers, or family don't see the possibilities that you (and the people you are working with) can. It requires you to silence the noise that only sees a place of deficits and to highlight the assets and opportunities that encourage so many to work hard for change. It requires honoring what is and working for what can and should be through shared vision developed in community with others.

As a college student, I was introduced to a definition for the work of *community engagement* that I hope inspires you as it has me. Nadinne Cruz, a pioneer in higher education community engagement and a person who embodies full and active engagement with the people, problems, and promises of a community, has defined this process as "combining intention and action in a move towards more just relationships" (Cruz, 1994). This idea of combining intention and action is a reminder that why we are there, what we hope to accomplish, and what we do in support of those aims matter. It is a reminder that we have an opportunity through this community engagement experience to help realize a more just community. It is a space that allows us to practice and perfect the work to be in and of community in ways that do not perpetuate and compound the injustice and marginalization already experienced.

Cruz's definition reflects Lee Anne Bell's (2007) dual-focused understanding of social justice: process and goal. The goal of community engagement practice should be the realization of more just relationships, which lead to a more just community, which leads to a more just world. But to realize that aim requires process—an ongoing engagement, trial and error, combining intention and action, working collaboratively—toward relationships that are equitable, inclusive, affirming, and cognizant of the capacity, agency, and dignity of every person.

As colleges and universities strive to "square [their] standards" to ensure their graduates are prepared to contribute fully and actively in our increasingly diverse democracy, community-engaged learning experiences have become an important strategy. And this book, particularly, seeks to make your community engagement experience a process that may lead to more just relationships in the communities where this work happens. The intentions, imperatives, dispositions, and responsibilities that define a process of community engagement are necessary to work toward the more just world we seek.

May this experience of community engagement inspire you toward full and active engagement with the people, problems, and promises of the community where you live now and the communities you will consider yours in the future.

Tania D. Mitchell
Associate Professor
College of Education and Human Development
University of Minnesota

ACKNOWLEDGMENTS

This book would not have been possible without the insight, wisdom, support, suggestions, and love of many people. We want to thank Tania D. Mitchell and Chris Nayve for agreeing to write the foreword and afterword to this book. They have inspired us—and many others in the fields of service-learning and community-engaged learning—with their thoughtfulness and dedication to social justice. We are grateful to Elizabeth Dausch, the filmmaker responsible for the videos of our University of San Francisco students, faculty, staff, and community partners who was able to take our ideas about community-engaged learning and provide a vision of what that looked like on film. Thank you to everyone who agreed to be on camera for our videos. Our student stars include Presley Attardo, Kristian Balgobin, Anthony Bettencourt, Mary Cruz, Lionell Daggs III, Amanda Geraldo, Greta Karisny, Kimberly Kollwitz, Daniel Leon, Dylan Moore, Jacqline Murillo, and Bayli Tucker. Our community partner stars include Sam Dennison from Faithful Fools Ministry and Nico Bremond from Magic Zone and Collective Impact. Thank you, Professor Stephanie Sears, our faculty star.

We want to acknowledge everyone who read various versions of the manuscript at different steps along the way to this book. Thank you to Anna Richert and Greta Karisny, who gave the entire manuscript a careful read and provided valuable feedback at the end. We also want to thank the Advocates for Community Engagement at the McCarthy Center, including Nell Bayliss, Alejandro Cuevas, Amanda Geraldo, Alexa Gonzalez, Sonia Hurtado Ureno, Greta Karisny, Kiana Martinez, Vivienne Pismarov, Miriam Uribe, Chiweta Uzoka, and Nichole Vasquez, who read the proposal for this book and provided good advice after reading early versions of the first two chapters. Their insight helped shape our subsequent writing.

We want to express gratitude to students, faculty, and staff at the University of San Francisco who over the years have worked with us and demonstrated the dispositions we describe in this book: open-mindedness, humility, intellectual curiosity, empathy, and commitment. Further, we are grateful to our colleagues at the Leo T. McCarthy Center for Public Service and the Common Good. We feel incredibly fortunate to work with colleagues who exemplify the best of community engagement, who unstintingly share their knowledge, and who are generous in creating space for all of us to learn from each other. We know our own growth as community-engaged teachers would not be possible without their example.

Finally, Star is especially grateful to her spouse, Andrew, and her kids, Jackson and Stella, for encouraging her to take on this new and exciting scholarly challenge and supporting her in carving out time on evenings and weekends to think, research, and write. Star would also like to thank her coauthor for taking a very big leap of faith by embarking on this creative journey together and mentoring her through the process.

David is also grateful to family, friends, and partner Daniel for patience when the laptop came out even on the loveliest weekend afternoon. I can't promise it will never happen again, but I promise there will be a break! Thank you to Star for being a true scholarly partner from the beginning of this book to the end.

INTRODUCTION

Intentions: The Role of the *Student Companion* in Community-Engaged Learning

In a recent podcast a woman was recounting a story from her childhood. She described a summer when she was 9 years old when her dad tried to teach her to swim by literally throwing her into the deep end of the pool. The woman described the sense of initial shock and panic that came over her in the moments after she hit the water, coupled with (somewhat surprising) feelings of embarrassment and resentment. She recalled that she flailed for a while, staying afloat long enough to notice her dad's look of disapproval before sinking below the surface. Moments later, her dad reached in and pulled her out without saying a word, and that was the end of the swim lesson for the day. Later that night, she recalled overhearing her dad tell her mom, "I just don't understand why she didn't swim!"

This story struck a chord because jumping into community-engaged learning is like being thrown into the deep end of a pool. For many students (not all, and we'll elaborate on this further in a moment), community-engaged learning may require them to enter spaces they never knew existed and connect with people they haven't previously encountered. Just like dropping into a deep pool can be disorienting for those who have never swam before, going into a community that is very different from one's own can be disorienting, too. This is especially true when the community is struggling against the effects of systematic oppression and marginalization, and when the student has had limited prior experience with such communities. It's important to note that the converse is also true: Many students who come from marginalized groups and communities often feel as though navigating college is a sink-or-swim endeavor that requires them to deploy skills and knowledge that may not have been explicitly cultivated in their educational formation and lived reality.

In this case, community-engaged learning courses might be like diving into a familiar pool. These courses may provide an opportunity for students to return to their own communities or ones that are similar in terms of demographics, culture, or geography. Students returning to familiar community spaces may experience a range of feelings from excitement to apprehension to resistance. Some students talk about how their community-engaged courses helped them develop a sense of home away from home, whereas others feel they struggled to get out of their community and don't want to have to re-enter oppressive spaces. Whatever their feelings associated with community engagement, students who are from underserved communities or marginalized groups tend to be able to draw on specific relevant skills and knowledge that they've honed through lived experience. In chapter 3 we will talk about community cultural wealth (Yosso, 2005) as a set of competencies that allow racially minoritized students, in particular, to navigate higher education successfully. However, although particular students might be more familiar with social justice issues because of their own lived experience, that doesn't mean they should be expected to speak on behalf of a particular group or community.

This book is written for you—the student embarking on a community-engaged course experience. It is meant to honor you (and all students) by recognizing that each person is a unique amalgam of multiple identities, including (but not limited to) socioeconomic status, race, ethnicity, gender, and sexual orientation (Abrams & Hogg, 1990; Adams, 2000; McIntosh, 1988; Tajfel, 2010). Understanding diversity as a "given," we attempt to resist assumptions about what makes someone the "typical" or "ideal" community-engaged learning student and instead provide relevant and accessible information that can be used by diverse students to illuminate new ways of thinking about, and acting in, the world.

Now, back to our swimming metaphor. We can imagine that, at the most basic level, staying afloat in a pool requires knowledge of how to hold one's breath and application of basic kicking and paddling skills. With regard to community engagement, the equivalent basic knowledge and skills might include understanding the geography and demographics of the neighborhood and utilizing skills like interpersonal communication and navigation of public transportation systems. At the very least, these skills should allow you to reach your destination, a host organization or other site for engagement. Of course, just as one can learn and apply more advanced skills and knowledge in the act of swimming (think breathing techniques, butterfly strokes, and kick turns), students can develop and implement more advanced skills and knowledge that allow them to engage more meaningfully and impactfully with the community (think self-reflection skills, community organizing techniques, and knowledge of power dynamics).

In the podcast, the girl's father seemed frustrated and surprised that she didn't immediately start swimming when he threw her into the pool but instead panicked and flailed. To set her up for success, he should have prepared her by providing safety information and practicing basic skills with her. In the same way, instructors of community-engaged courses should not expect students to make their first foray into community without preparation. In fact, ensuring students exhibit open-mindedness, empathy, and commitment necessitates more than "jumping in." Fostering these dispositions requires modeling, reflecting on, and practicing them. Whether one expects a student to learn to swim or do community engagement, it is incumbent upon an instructor to teach the skills and knowledge necessary to do so effectively.

This book will help you develop and deploy the necessary skills and knowledge to participate in effective community-engaged learning. To be clear, when we talk about community-engaged learning, we mean a course-based experience that cultivates your academic and civic knowledge and skills, as well as values and commitments, through direct engagement with communities and groups working to overcome systemic injustice. Engagement might look like direct service (think tutoring or serving meals), advocacy or activism (think registering voters or participating in organized demonstrations), participatory action research (think administering surveys or collecting oral histories to inform community change efforts), or simple solidarity (think talking and listening to people describe their struggles to resist oppression and honoring their lived experience). Although doing community-engaged learning isn't a life-or-death situation in the way staying afloat in a deep swimming pool is, the experience does entail high stakes. It's remarkably easy for students to inadvertently do harm if they aren't mindful about how their actions can impact others. That harm might translate into individuals feeling disrespected and dehumanized or into entire organizations wasting resources and time to work with students only to discover that the project they needed wasn't completed. Assuming you and your instructor want to avoid such issues, think of this book as the companion that will coach you through those first few toe-dips into the deep end of the community engagement pool.

We begin by setting the context for our work of community engagement. Each of us can probably identify a justice issue that directly affects us or people we love, or at least an issue that we witness playing out on a daily basis and care deeply about. We know that these issues are complicated and not easy to solve. Chapter 1 provides information on just how pervasive and complex some of these issues are. In addition to providing critical contextual information, this chapter is meant to spark a sense of urgency to act, and to help you start thinking about how your community-engaged course connects with these issues.

Chapter 2 then speaks to why community-engaged learning is a valuable way to acquire, analyze, and apply new learning because it allows students to organically navigate authentic contexts. Through this chapter, we explore the power of learning by doing, the possibility of opening up your worldview by interacting with diverse individuals, and the ways you can function as a teacher as well as a learner. Further, community-engaged learning has the power to move you and your peers toward informed and effective community action. You'll be interacting with, and learning from, community residents and change-makers. Instead of peeking out the windows of your ivory tower (a common metaphor for colleges and universities) and observing social justice issues from afar, you will be engaging those issues at ground level to analyze their root causes, symptoms, impacts, and interventions.

To prepare you for this dynamic learning experience, in chapter 3 we've curated some unique insights and advice from those involved in community-engaged learning, including students, alumni, faculty, community partners, and community members. We'll suggest dispositions that set you up to maximize your learning *and* your contribution to community change efforts. Although it is said that "the road to hell is paved with good intentions," being mindful about your intentions related to community engagement is a necessary first step in getting beyond that (seemingly low) bar of "do no harm" so you can act in ways that benefit the community.

To accompany these new ways of thinking, we provide advice on how to put your values and dispositions into practice in chapter 4. This is where we are going to get really concrete. What should you do when you enter your host organization for the first time? How should you interact with the organization's staff, volunteers, and clients? What clues can you pick up about the culture and values of the organization or broader community just by being observant? How do you operationalize "professionalism"? What does it mean to "unpack" uncomfortable community-engaged experiences? Don't worry! You'll find the answers to all of these questions if you just keep reading.

In chapter 5, this book ends by introducing you to case studies of students who have experienced the transformative power of community-engaged learning. These stories illustrate common themes inherent in the student experience, including listening to understand, challenging stereotypes, learning your role, and seeing the world through a new lens. Our hope is that these stories inspire you to orchestrate your own transformation through community engagement.

Note that we've integrated a special feature into this book. You can scan embedded QR codes in most of the chapters to explore particular themes and perspectives more deeply. In some cases, the code will take you to a video intended for public viewing (on YouTube or Vimeo). Please be aware that public content on many media sites is open to viewer comments that are not reviewed, curated, or edited. Some of the comments may be inflammatory and offensive, so we encourage you to avoid reading them and focus on the content in the videos. In other cases, you'll access original video content that we produced specifically to accompany this companion book. If you don't already have one, you can download a QR code reader onto your smart phone. The QR code reader app is easy to use, and new users can walk through the app's instructions to learn how to scan the codes in the book.

You'll also notice that we've woven critical questions into each chapter to prompt you to reflect on the ideas and perspectives presented in this book. When you come across these questions, we suggest that you read them and then process your thinking through writing or peer discussion. In fact, it's a great idea to frequently discuss themes and questions from this book, as well as insights about your community-engaged experiences, with classmates, community partners, and your instructor. Our hope is that you enter into your community-engaged learning experience, and this book, with intellectual curiosity, critical consideration, a desire to contribute to the common good of your community, and a commitment to building authentic relationships across differences.

I

IMPERATIVES

Why We Do Community-Engaged Learning

All too often we think of community in terms of being with folks like ourselves: the same class, same race, same ethnicity, same social standing and the like. I think we need to be wary: we need to work against the danger of evoking something that we don't challenge ourselves to actually practice.

—bell hooks, *Teaching Community: A Pedagogy of Hope*

Community is that place where the person you least want to live with always lives. And when that person moves away, someone else arises to take his or her place.

—Parker J. Palmer, "Community, Conflict, and Ways of Knowing: Ways to Deepen Our Educational Agenda"

Every single person has capabilities, abilities and gifts. Living a good life depends on whether those capabilities can be used, abilities expressed and gifts given. If they are, the person will be valued, feel powerful and well-connected to the people around them. And the community around the person will be more powerful because of the contribution the person is making.

—John P. Kretzmann and John L. McKnight, *Building Communities from the Inside Out*

As you begin your community-engaged learning project, think about the three quotations that serve as epigraphs for this chapter. How do you define *community*? How do these quotations support or challenge you to think differently about community? What surprises you about how they frame your relationship to the community? Do they make you excited about learning in community? Perhaps a little nervous? Some of both? What opportunities and challenges are evoked?

If you are feeling mixed emotions, you are probably in an appropriate frame of mind to enter a community-engaged learning experience. We believe that, overall, you will find that the opportunities more than balance the challenges and the positive emotions replace any initial concerns. As the hooks quotation implies, you will have opportunities to grow by encountering difference, challenging preconceived notions, bringing your most open mind, and working to understand the experiences, wisdom, and insight of others. hooks reminds us that community engagement requires acknowledging our identity and the identities of those we meet in community. Follow the link in Figure 1.1 and listen to the first 1:10 minutes to hear bell hooks expand on this idea in her own life.

Figure 1.1. bell hooks on community.

Note: See video at www.youtube.com/watch?v=EjRSk4hlrtI

Palmer is not speaking about community-engaged learning, but he does foreshadow how community engagement involves work; how community is an ongoing process, not just an unchanging thing; and how learning in community—and potentially encountering difficult differences along the way—is not always easy. Kretzmann and McKnight point out to us why all this work is worthwhile. You have not only the opportunity to be the person using capabilities and giving of your talents but also the chance to benefit from others in the community doing the same and be part of the more powerful community.

Compare that to sitting in a lecture hall, listening to someone run through a PowerPoint presentation for 50 minutes and taking notes silently. Not that you can't learn something in a lecture hall, but you're not going to have the experience described in the opening quotations. It's why you are lucky to be in a community-engaged learning course. You may not have been thinking of all this when you signed up for such a course. Your instructor has assigned this book, however, because he or she knows that entering into and learning from community require preparation. This book is designed to prepare you for that community-engaged learning, not only so you get the most out of it but also so your community partner also benefits. You will realize that learning from community is a process that requires authenticity—meaning you know yourself, including your strengths and your weaknesses, and are open to learning from and respectful of others—and reciprocity—meaning you are in a relationship where you gain as much as give, learn as much as serve.

As you read this and other chapters, we will present you with information and perspectives that may be new to you. Information is more than just something to know. It is also something that makes us feel. We acknowledge that reading about the inequalities and injustices of the world that serve as imperatives for community engagement can make us angry or sad, activated or resistant. We are whole people—hearts and guts and souls and brains—when we enter community-engaged learning. Your emotions and understanding of self are as important as what you learn about the world around you.

The perspectives that inform this book come from our critical lens for understanding inequality and injustice. These perspectives help us understand why racism and poverty have been persistent, why inequalities have consistently privileged whiteness and wealth, and why charity alone only alleviates symptoms of these problems but never makes them go away. We know that for some of you, this critical perspective already informs how you see the world. For others, it may give you new language to understand concepts that you have always understood at some level. And for others still, this critical lens may be new and challenging. For those encountering and perhaps struggling with these ideas for the first time, we ask you to bring an open mind.

Throughout, we will prompt you with questions, and we hope you will indulge us by grappling with them. The first prompt for reflection asks you to complete this sentence: I do community-engaged learning because . . .

Although we acknowledge that going to school is, in part, about meeting requirements, our hope is that you did not answer this question by saying, "Because I'm required to." If you are doing community-engaged learning because your college or professor is requiring it, let's look at why this might be required. Your college may have a community engagement or service-learning requirement because it believes part of its job is preparing students not only for a personally meaningful life and a promising job but also for life in democratic communities. Community engagement and service-learning put you in the middle of working with diverse individuals, groups, and organizations committed to making a difference in the world with integrity and thoughtfulness. This is not just preparation for democratic life, it is actually engaging in it, something educational philosopher John Dewey (1916) reminds us is central to the mission of schools. Your college may require community engagement as a way to carry out its mission for social justice. If that is the case, you will want to think of your work as not only a requirement but also an opportunity to do something that makes the world more equal and just and that provides you with a perspective to make this work a commitment in your life. Perhaps your college or university wants you to develop a sense of belongingness, and community engagement is another way to "belong" to a larger community beyond the one on campus. Community-engaged learning may be a way to engage with people you previously viewed as "outside" your community. In that case, carry a mind-set of openness to meeting and learning from others. Finally, your school may see community engagement as a means to make learning relevant and lasting. The phrase *book learning* is rarely used in a complimentary way, and your community engagement is a chance to go beyond holding abstract and inert knowledge.

Getting beyond "it's required," try to revisit your answer to the prompt, "I do community-engaged learning because . . ." What if you were to consider other possible answers to that question? To get you thinking of those possibilities, think about a social, political, or environmental issue that you may have been involved with previously or that you care about. Reflect on how you first encountered the issue. Consider your own motivations, relationships, and other factors that guided you to get involved or care. What emerged from your involvement with the issue? Think in terms of new learning and relationships. What do you see as some of the takeaways or lessons learned from that occasion to remember as you enter this new community-engaged learning experience? If you haven't been involved in any issues or even if you have and want to challenge yourself to get involved in new areas, watch a short 1-minute video (Figure 1.2) of students answering why they are doing community-engaged learning. The examples in this video can help you brainstorm issues to which you feel connected.

Figure 1.2. Students on the imperatives of community-engaged learning.

Note: See video at https://vimeo.com/236989824/ce3ab44db9

Notice that these students found reasons outside themselves for why they do community-engaged learning. But unlike the answer "because it's required," which is also external, their answers were motivated by a desire to address the problems they describe. These are the imperatives to community-engaged learning.

It's worth considering more deeply the reasons they mention. Each one is reason alone to take action. Taken together, they make us realize that our planet is at a tipping point of sustainability and our society at a crucial moment in its viability. Clearly we are called to engage, and our education gives us privilege that makes our engagement even more necessary. If you are not convinced yet, consider some of these additional data that call us to action.

Underrepresentation of Women and People of Color in Government Leadership and Decision-Making

We all know the record of women and people of color who have served as president of the United States. We may know less about the Senate and House of Representatives. Of the 10,000 persons who have served in the House of Representatives since 1789, fewer than 300 have been women. Of the 2,000 who have served in the Senate in that same time period, only 50 have been women. And although things are better now than in 1789, only 21 of the 100 senators in the 115th Congress are women. In the three most recent Congresses, 19% of representatives in the House have been women (Center for American Women and Politics, 2018).

In terms of race and ethnicity, the 115th Congress is the most diverse ever, but it is still more than 80% White. Non-White elected officials include 50 African Americans, 39 Hispanic Americans, 15 Asian Americans, and 2 Native Americans. Twenty (or 34%) of the 59 persons elected to Congress for the first time in 2016 were people of color. By contrast, only 11 (or 15%) of the 71 persons elected for the first time in 2014 were people of color. At the same time, the 106 people of color in the 115th Congress represent only 20% of officials serving in that body. This percentage compares to the 38% of people of color in the United States. Although the percentage of people of color has increased from 12% in the 107th Congress elected in 2000, so has the percentage of people of color, which has grown from 31% at that time, meaning the gap in representation has only grown wider (Bialik & Krogstad, 2017).

Not all important decisions are made in government. We live in a time when public investment in education and social support is shrinking and where markets are valorized as the best way to allocate resources, including labor, financial capital, and natural resources. This system is called *neoliberalism* because it places freedom to make economic decisions, including decisions by corporations, as a paramount concern over other kinds of freedoms, for example, freedom from poverty. Indeed, in the 2010 decision *Citizens United* the Supreme Court ruled that corporations have the right to spend unlimited amounts of money on elections because that spending is a form of free speech protected under the First Amendment. In such a world, the decisions made by corporations have wide-reaching impact and threaten to overwhelm individual and collective public voices.

Who heads these corporations? Among the CEOs of Fortune 500 companies, only 21 are women (Zarya, 2016). Only 15 African Americans have ever become the CEO of a Fortune 500 company (Black Chairmen, n.d.). Media businesses reflect similar inequalities. Women hold fewer than 7% of radio and television licenses. People of color hold slightly more than 7% of radio licenses and 3% of television licenses (Free Press, n.d.). At print newspapers, 17% of journalists are people of color, and 38% are women. At online-only news organizations, 23% of journalists are people of color, and 50% are women (American Society of News Editors, 2016). As we've been seeing in the news, the tech industry, which is much vaunted as an engine of economic growth in the United States, employs disproportionate numbers of Whites, Asian Americans, and men (Davidson, 2016).

Educational Inequity

Disparities in investment in education for children across different racial and economic groups represent what writer Jonathan Kozol (1991) termed *savage inequalities*. Reflecting the resources that their communities can contribute to schools, students in wealthy suburbs of some metropolitan areas like Chicago and New York are likely to receive more than twice as much in additional funding for their education compared to students in city schools. As might be expected, these inequalities in investment result in inequalities in educational outcomes. These are not surprising; indeed, they are predictable. Disparities in school achievement occur in patterns that are recognizable, predictable, and preventable. Currently, 76% of Black students and 79% of Hispanic students graduate on time, compared to 88% of White students and 91% of Asian/Pacific Islander students (Balingit, 2017).

Inequalities start early. Although 19% of preschool students are Black, they account for 47% of preschool expulsions. Preschool expulsions, often driven by implicit racial bias, pathologize normal childhood behavior and force parents to find other preschool options. Inequalities that begin in preschool extend into college and graduate school. Students of color make up only 25% of the

PhDs granted in the United States, and although women have made great strides in higher education, they are still underrepresented in all STEM fields except biology (Matson, 2013; National Center for Education Statistics, n.d.).

The school-to-prison pipeline is a pernicious aspect of educational inequity. The pipeline refers to the phenomenon of moving students of color and economically poor students out of school and into the juvenile or adult justice system. Zero tolerance policies in schools that push students into the criminal justice system for the smallest infractions contribute to criminalizing what in wealthier schools serving mostly White students would be handled as in-school discipline problems (American Civil Liberties Union, 2018).

The story in Figure 1.3 (an 8-minute audio clip) describes how the school-to-prison pipeline works in the nation's largest public school system.

Figure 1.3. School-to-prison pipeline.

Note: Go to www.wnyc.org/story/blocking-school-prison-pipeline/ for audio

Racial Resegregation

Perhaps you are already familiar with the phenomenon of gentrification—the process by which the property values and demographics of a neighborhood change as poor people, artists, people of color, and small independent businesses are forced out of a neighborhood when it becomes popular with wealthier, predominantly White people. Although cities like Brooklyn and San Francisco are well-known examples, this process affects many cities, large and small, throughout the country. You may go to school in a city or town with a "hot" neighborhood full of expensive cafés, galleries, boutiques, and new or renovated apartments. Those developments are considered a sign of gentrification. As a city or neighborhood gentrifies, it becomes less diverse and, ironically, loses the qualities that made it "hot" in the first place.

Resegregation today looks different from the "White flight" from cities in the second half of the twentieth century. It is slower but no less widespread. As a recent study points out, as neighborhoods change from one racial or ethnic group to another, they will appear integrated for a time but resegregate eventually. Unlike the past, White people do not move out of cities as they did in the White flight of the later twentieth century. Rather, they tend to move into specific city neighborhoods, with the characteristics previously described, resulting in a slower form of urban resegregation that is happening in cities like New York, Los Angeles, Chicago, and Houston (Bader & Warkentien, 2016).

Gentrification and segregation are not inevitable. Suburbs today are more integrated than in the last century when covenants in deeds to houses prevented owners from selling to anyone other than Whites and when banks "redlined" neighborhoods, restricting people of color to only certain neighborhoods when they sought a mortgage to buy a house. Today's integration is fragile (Orfield, 2002), but some cities provide examples of urban development without displacement of poor people, immigrants, and people of color. To learn about a neighborhood in Oakland that is working to develop without gentrification, watch the film in Figure 1.4 (11 minutes), which was created by students as part of a community-engaged learning project.

Figure 1.4. Sustaining community without gentrification.

Note: See video at www.youtube.com/watch?v=QXjjaogothM

Food Insecurity

According to the U.S. Department of Agriculture (2017), 14% of all households are *food insecure*, which is defined as being "uncertain of having, or unable to acquire, enough food to meet the needs of all their members because they had insufficient money or other resources." That adds up to more than 48 million people in the United States. Despite social safety nets, food insecurity disproportionately affects children and seniors. Food insecurity is worse in rural areas than in urban areas, an irony considering that many rural families grow or process food (USDA Economic Research Service, 2017). It also affects college students. Four out of 10 University of California students do not have access to nutritious food (Watanabe & Newell, 2016). Wherever poverty exists, food insecurity is a consequence, as illustrated in the film in Figure 1.5 (6:21 minutes).

Figure 1.5.   Food insecurity.

Note: See video at www.youtube.com/watch?v=aB6rX51ub30

In urban areas, *food deserts*, or places without supermarkets where it is difficult to find nutritious and fresh food, contribute to food insecurity as poor families pay more for groceries at corner stores with limited selections of food.

No Living Wage

A living wage is the amount of money required in a locality to lead a life of dignity. Currently, the federal minimum wage is US$7.25 an hour, an amount far short of what is considered a living wage in many places. Even when working more than one full-time job at minimum wage, some individuals may still need financial assistance. In some cities and states, the minimum is higher to reflect the higher cost of living. If you are wondering how much it costs to live where you are, use the link in Figure 1.6 to the Living Wage Calculator at the Massachusetts Institute of Technology. You can check on what constitutes a living wage by locality.

Figure 1.6. Calculating a living wage.

Note: See calculator at http://livingwage.mit.edu

You may very well know what it is like to live on minimum wage. If you do not, the clip in Figure 1.7 (6:40 minutes) will help you understand.

Figure 1.7. Living on minimum wage.

Note: See video at www.youtube.com/watch?v=-SCB1t28nDU or www.youtube.com/watch?v=h-UosVZ4gk8

In contrast to the minimum wage, in 2016, your service for community-engaged learning was valued on average at more than US$24 per hour by Independent Sector (2016), an organization that calculates what volunteers contribute to their local communities across the United States. Discrepancies between living wages and real wages raise questions about the value of labor and whether wages reflect that value. For example, as a society, we believe young people are our future, yet early childhood educators working with those young people are poorly paid.

State Brutality Against People of Color

Few injustices have led to more recent activism by young people across the country than the killing of unarmed Black men by police. Such examples include the following:

- Eric Garner; New York City; July 17, 2014
- Michael Brown; Ferguson, Missouri; August 9, 2014
- Tamir Rice; Cleveland, Ohio; November 22, 2014
- Walter Scott; North Charleston, South Carolina; April 4, 2015
- Freddie Gray; Baltimore, Maryland; April 19, 2015
- Alton Sterling; Baton Rouge, Louisiana; July 5, 2016
- Philando Castile; Falcon Heights, Minnesota; July 6, 2016
- Stephon Clark; Sacramento, California; March 18, 2018

These names are part of a long historical injustice of using state power to maintain White supremacy. Their deaths spawned several movements, including Black Lives Matter. Although each of these deaths has caused much pain, loss, and anger, the last three, posted on social media, sparked particular outrage, reminding the nation of the danger that Black and brown people face in their own communities at the hands of law enforcement. We know police work is difficult and honorable. We also know that racial bias influences police officers' decisions on the job (Gelman, Fagan, & Kiss, 2007). Seeing these shootings online raises questions about what we do at the local level to prevent such brutality. What do our beliefs about moral justice compel us to do as a nation?

Losing Wildlife Faster Than Ever

Currently, more than 13,000 species are listed as critically endangered by the International Union for Conservation of Nature (2017). The World Wildlife Fund (2016) estimates that the number of wild animals on the planet has been cut by more than half in the last 40 years. The main reasons for this loss include human exploitation, habitat change and loss, and climate change. In 2016, the planet saw its first extinction tied to global warming: the Bramble Cay melomys, a rodent that lived on a tiny outcrop of Australia's Great Barrier Reef and was wiped out by rising tides (Innis, 2016). In the future, one in six species could face extinction from climate change (Urban, 2015).

Stigma of Mental Illness

Mental illness is treatable, and having a mental illness does not need to prevent anyone from participating meaningfully in life. However, because of biases in society and the lack of comprehensive services, persons with mental illnesses face more than only medical problems. They must deal with accessing health care in a nation where it is not always readily available or culturally appropriate, meaning it meets not only medical needs but also the social, cultural, and linguistic needs of patients. They also face discrimination in employment and housing that can lead to a host of other problems, including unemployment and homelessness. More than 124,000—or one-fifth—of the 610,000 homeless people across the United States suffer from mental illnesses like schizophrenia, depression, or bipolar disorder according to the Department of Housing and Urban Development, as reported by *USA Today* (Jervis, 2014). Living on the streets with a mental illness poses all kinds of threats, the most serious being death from causes ranging from violence to exposure. This is the result of the stigma of mental illness.

As authors of this book, we struggle with sharing these statistics and portraits of social and environmental ills with you. We know that for some, these data could be overwhelming. For others, we worry that these data could reinforce stereotypes about people and the individual causes of poverty. We hope, however, that they inspire you to look further into issues that call you to action and provide a context for making sense of your community-engaged learning. That context is one of social structural factors that shape inequality and injustice in our world. We know that individuals make choices and some of those result in personal hardship. We also know that people operate in larger social, political, and economic systems. Those systems do not affect everyone equally, as you can see. Not everyone has to make decisions about buying food versus paying for health care. Not everyone questions if she will be taken seriously as a candidate for elected office because of her gender. Not everyone worries in the same way about being pulled over by a police officer. These differences affecting people unequally shape what kinds of choices some of us make.

Sometimes these larger social systems causing such injustice are called *structural inequality,* meaning the inequality results from a stacked deck presenting limited options among bad choices that some people, often because of race and class, are forced to make. Consider homelessness. The sociologist Matthew Desmond (2016) has documented how economic and legal systems are structured in such a way that some people, especially poor, single women of color, are constantly forced to deal with housing insecurity and make choices that work against moving to more stable housing situations.

Many of the issues described in this chapter intersect. For example, educational inequities intersect with neighborhood segregation, which both connect to unequal political and economic representation. Seeing these intersections allows us to understand the complexities of seeking social change. Although we may work on one particular issue, our efforts can have impact beyond that. What we want you to understand from this is that in your community-engaged work, you may be helping individuals dealing with injustice, but do not lose sight of the systems in the larger world that are causing injustice. Realize that your work in the community matters not only for your education but also the lives of others.

Like the students in the video, think about the issues that matter to you. How can you engage one of those issues in particular? How can you take the information about inequality and injustice presented so far and use it to understand your community-engaged work? Can you frame your work in the community positively? In other words, can you think less in terms of what the scholar Eve Tuck (2009) calls *damage-centered work* and more in terms of *desire-centered work*? Often motivated by a sense of social justice and seeking change, damage-centered work is focused on what is not working and what is wrong in the lives of individuals and communities. It can inadvertently reinforce notions of people and communities as broken. By contrast, desire-centered work focuses on the vision and wisdom in people and communities. It provides possibilities for action based on what might be or what once was. If you focus on an issue in a damage-centered way, you run the risk of looking at people only as suffering from that problem, not as complex, nuanced individuals dealing with a problem but also so much more. You may have thought only in terms of solving one person's problem rather than thinking about how a community of people would make a larger change. Consider how your community-engaged work can draw on collective vision and build something, not merely ameliorate part of a problem.

The last person in the first video clip you watched says she is afraid of becoming desensitized. How did you react to thinking about these issues after reading the statistics in this chapter? Desensitized? Overwhelmed? Helpless? Aware? Motivated? Capable? Our hope is that you do not become desensitized. We understand that becoming used to injustice can mean doing less to change it. Our media are full of people who, because they are aware, motivated, and capable, are not desensitized, who take action for change. We hope that by being present, authentic, and reflective, you continue to feel mobilized rather than desensitized.

Think of Alicia Garza, who was angered at the shooting death of Trayvon Martin, an unarmed 17-year-old Black young man, and at the 2013 acquittal of the man accused of killing him. Garza wrote a post on Facebook saying that "black lives matter" (Guynn, 2015). As special projects director at the National Domestic Workers Alliance, Garza understood the importance of organizing. Her friend Patrice Cullors understood the power of the Internet and created the hashtag from Garza's words. Opal Tometi built the online platform. Together they started a movement challenging racism that has resonated across college campuses as well as communities throughout the United States (Garza, 2014).

Think of pediatrician Mona Hanna-Attisha, who began testing for environmental toxins when she learned that Flint, Michigan, was not doing anything to check levels of lead in drinking water after switching its water source from Lake Huron to the polluted Flint River. Her data showed that lead was contaminating the city's water. Despite denials from city and state officials, she pressed forward until government agencies confirmed her findings and took responsibility (Erb, 2015).

Garza and Hanna-Attisha did not succumb to desensitization. Instead they felt that injustice called them to work with others to make change. As we are writing this book, young activists are protesting revocation of Deferred Action for Childhood Arrivals (DACA) for approximately 800,000 people who came to the United States before they were 16 years old. Revoking DACA would mean these young people could be deported. Here again, young people are responding with action to injustice. Young people are also protesting gun violence in schools and communities. This chapter takes its title, "Imperatives," because what it describes are urgent, important issues that move people to action. Look for the imperatives that move you in your community-engaged learning and can help set a course for your life using your education for the common good.

BENEFITS

What We Gain From Community-Engaged Learning

Beyond the reasons for community engagement that are about making a difference in the world, there are also reasons that are personal, that are about what you gain. What do you hope to gain from your community-engaged learning? If you said a good grade, perhaps you were being cynical. But if we reframe getting a good grade, we can also think of it as one way of acknowledging that when our work really matters, we are called to do our best. So, of course, you should get a good grade. But more important, you should want to do your best work because the community you are working with deserves no less.

Watch the short video in Figure 2.1 (1:26 minutes) to learn about some of the personal benefits from community-engaged learning.

Figure 2.1. Students on the imperatives of community-engaged learning.

Note: See video at https://vimeo.com/236989704/cae21acae7

How do the students' reasons help you understand what you might gain from community-engaged learning? We hope that many of these benefits will resonate with you. The reasons mentioned bear further consideration.

I See My Community in New Ways

Too often communities are portrayed as broken, lacking, or troubled. This is a deficit notion of community. Headlines about problems like crime and poverty in a community contribute to deficit thinking. When these images and headlines are about our own community, we know they are not the whole story. Yet even people living in a community are sometimes forced to think in terms of deficits. For example, when making the case for new policy, community activists often have to base their appeal to lawmakers on the needs of their community rather than its strengths. In contrast, community-engaged learning can orient us toward seeing the assets of a community. What are the funds of knowledge, the ways of knowing and understanding that draw on a community's strengths and wisdom? What is the cultural wealth, the art, the stories, the history that exists in the community? What are the ideas, insights, and webs of relationship that exist in the community? What members of the community are leading and contributing to positive change? This shift to ask questions about a community's assets can change the way we enter a community. It can help us see value in places where framing by some media or politicians may too often focus on problems (Kretzman & McKnight, 1993).

It Informs the Way I Engage With the World

Do you understand the causes and responses to social injustice? Do you see yourself as capable of changing the world for the better? Do you see yourself as called to engage? A good community-engaged learning experience helps you develop the knowledge, skills, and dispositions to engage with the world and leave it a better place.

It Makes Me a Better Student

Better can mean a lot of things, but in this case, it means more aware and a critical thinker. Research shows that service-learning, a type of community-engaged learning, is an example of a "high-impact practice" (American Association of Colleges & Universities, 2018) that gives meaning to course work and creates greater awareness of diversity. High-impact practices also contribute positively to critical thinking and are seen as contributing to student success in college (Kilgo, Ezell Sheets, & Pascarella, 2015). A study by Eyler, Giles, and Braxton (1997) found that students in service-learning courses gained confidence to make a difference as citizens and believed they improved in the skills necessary to make that difference. They gained empathy and open-mindedness.

Because I Want to Contribute to the Good of Our Society

Community-engaged learning can help you think more deeply about defining and serving the common good. Is the common good the sum of each individual seeking to maximize his or her own best interests? That's what a market-driven approach to the common good would tell us. Or is it something that is shared, that benefits all, something that cannot be reduced to a commodity benefiting individuals solely? Your community-engaged learning course should help you develop an orientation toward serving the common good. In some cases, your contributions to the common good may be in the form of direct service, taking action to ameliorate the results of injustice. In other cases, your contribution may address the causes of injustice. Both kinds of action are necessary and valuable. As you reflect on your community-engaged learning, you will gain insight into where you feel called to make your contribution to the good of society.

Because I Learn From Agents of Change in My Community

Knowledge comes in lots of different forms. All that you are learning in the classroom contributes to your ability to theorize and critically analyze the world. What you gain from community-engaged learning, though, is wisdom from the experience of people living and working in the community, including those working to make the world more just and equitable. Learning at the side of community agents of change contributes to your development not only as a student but also as a participant and leader in democratic community life.

Because I Can Learn More Outside of the Classroom

Learning is more meaningful and more likely to last when it happens in a practical context. The community provides a place where we not only apply what we learn in classrooms but also where we reflect on action and develop our own theories to bring back to classroom discourse. This connection between theory and practice is called *praxis*, the cycle by which knowledge informs action and action informs knowledge. The community is also a site of learning, not just a place where we apply learning. Individuals and organizations will be your coteachers in community-engaged learning. The community is a source of wisdom with its own methods, purposes, and forms of knowledge.

It Helps Me Build Compassion for Myself and Other People

Empathy is an important trait and one that civic and political discourse could use more of. Community-engaged learning experiences have the potential to help us develop an ethic of care. They can teach us to be generous with others as we understand the world from their points of view and with ourselves as we understand our own identities and processes of becoming agents of change.

Community-engaged learning also develops our compassion for self. In fact, self-care and self-compassion are necessary as one works for social justice. In the process, you may find you make mistakes, inadvertently offend others, bump against biases you were not aware of, and face some of your own weaknesses. This is not easy, and it takes compassion for oneself to work through the discomfort that accompanies this personal dimension of learning. When people say that they got more out of community-engaged learning than they contributed to others, they are often referring to this powerful, personal understanding of self. Self-care and being gentle with oneself help us continue doing meaningful, long-lasting work.

I Believe It's Important to Live Out My Faith

Every faith tradition appeals to followers to serve others, and most religious organizations have community service branches or units devoted to service. Most places of worship are centers not only of worship but also of service to the community. Many of you may have had your first experience of community engagement through service as part of your religious education at a mosque, temple, or church.

Even if you are not a member of a religious faith, you may find some transcendent quality to service and community. According to a study conducted at UCLA, even as students' religious engagement declines, their spiritual qualities grow. Meeting people from diverse cultures and backgrounds through community-engaged learning contributes to students' understanding of others and of themselves and their spiritual growth. Reflection, a key characteristic of community-engaged learning, contributes to this growth as well (Astin et al., 2005).

The Skills and Knowledge That I Gain Will Help Me in My Career

Gaining career skills may not be the primary reason for community-engaged learning, but it is an important benefit. The attributes that employers most want to see in new college graduates include leadership, ability to work in a team, and communication skills. Community-engaged projects contribute to leadership development by giving you opportunities to work with others to meet their priorities and dreams. This is sometimes called servant leadership because this kind of leader puts the desires of others before his or her own. *Community-engaged learning* by definition involves working with others, and that requires strong collaboration skills. Community engagement calls us to collaborate with people who have very different ideas and work across what are sometimes competing agendas toward a common goal. Strong communication skills across differences in professional settings are highly valued by employers, and you will find yourself practicing this skill with other classmates and community partners (Adams, 2014).

I Build Relationships With People Who Live and Think Differently Than I Do

Community-engaged learning is about relationships, even if the logistics of community engagement—finding a community partner, logging hours, filling out evaluations—focuses us initially on roles. Roles can be limiting if we think only in terms of ourselves being in a position of serving. That puts those we work with in the position of being served, a position that is inherently unequal and less powerful. If we think of being in relationships that are not hierarchical or imbalanced, then serving and being served, learning and teaching are two-directional or reciprocal rather than one-way. These kinds of relationships model a just world. Beneficial relationships in community-engaged learning are also called authentic because they are based on mutuality and respect. They lead to greater feelings of connection with members of the community. These kind of relationships stand in contrast to transactional ones, where parties to a relationship expect to get something out of them but not be changed or transformed in the process.

The Community That I Came From Is the One I Serve

The reality for many of you reading this book is that when you leave the classroom for community-engaged learning, you are working in your own community. It may be the actual community where you live, or if you moved to a new city or town for college, you may find that the people in the community are similar to those with whom you identify or from where you came. That gives you insight into the particular community's wealth. If you do not, however, come from the community you serve, enter with humility that allows you to look for assets and learn from those who do know it well.

My Assumptions and Beliefs Are Challenged and I Get to Challenge Others

Community-engaged learning goes deep. Whereas some forms of teaching and learning lead to gaining new knowledge that is held only until it is tested, community-engaged learning has the potential to change not only the amount of what we know but also how and why we know things and how we use knowledge. When we challenge our assumptions and beliefs, we set ourselves up for changing our perspective on ourselves, others, and the world. When we build relationships rather than work in roles with others, we are much more open to such change. As discussed already, we can challenge the assumptions that some people have about communities as damaged places. We should challenge the uncritical assumption that service is always good. Although well-intentioned, some service-informing community engagement can have no impact or negative impacts. Our first commitment should always be to do no harm. We can do this by constantly challenging our assumptions and trusting the needs identified by the community.

It Empowers Me to Be an Agent of Change

What does it mean for you to be an agent of change? Who are the people you imagine when you think of agents of change? Are they people who seem larger than life, impossible to emulate, almost intimidating in their ability to single-handedly effect change? Consider how icons of change for social justice, like Rosa Parks or

Harvey Milk, have been presented in history books. For example, although it is inaccurate, you may have heard the story about Rosa Parks as a hero acting alone and on the spur of the moment who was too tired to give up her seat to a White man on a segregated bus. What that story obscures is that she was deeply involved in a movement with others, thinking strategically about how to dismantle segregation (Kohl, 2005). Similarly, Harvey Milk is often portrayed in textbooks as an individual coming from nowhere to win public office and speak on behalf of LGBT rights. That story hides his work to build diverse coalitions of people who saw the interconnections between the rights of one group and the rights of others, including their own (Donahue, 2014). Understanding the pathways taken by heroes like Parks and Milk reminds us that being an agent of change means working with others, taking actions that are part of something bigger, and seeing the long term as well as the moment. Think about how your community-engaged work for your course allows you to develop as this kind of agent of change. You can learn how to work in coalition with others, think strategically, and participate in movements rather than solo actions.

The video opening this chapter ended with a quotation from Uruguayan journalist, writer, and novelist, Eduardo Galeano:

> I don't believe in charity. I believe in solidarity. Charity is so vertical. It goes from the top to the bottom. Solidarity is horizontal. It respects the other person. I have a lot to learn from other people. (Barsamian, 2004, p. 146)

What does it mean that "charity is vertical" and "solidarity is horizontal"? Can you think of actions that align with notions of charity or solidarity? Thinking about being an agent of change, what do you have to learn from other people? The people you work with in community? The people, including your professor, in your class who reflect with you on community engagement? The people who write the books and articles assigned in your course? Share your list of what you have to learn and whom you can learn from with others. See how these lists build openness toward learning and contribute toward humility and the kind of solidarity about which Galeano writes.

3

DISPOSITIONS

Who We Are Called to Be as Community-Engaged Learners

Charity and solidarity, as described in the Eduardo Galeano quote in the previous chapter, are examples of human dispositions. Some scholars describe dispositions as filters, comprising people's values, beliefs, cultural backgrounds, cognitive processes, and prior experiences that shape how they take in new information and make meaning of the world around them (Schussler, 2006). Consider how an air filter is designed to remove particles and impurities so that the air has a more desirable composition. This is true of dispositional filters, which process information in a way that elicits particular behaviors and actions. To put it simply, dispositions determine what information you let in, how you make sense of it, and how you act on it. Each person has multiple dispositions that can converge, compete, or even conflict in a variety of ways in different contexts.

To provide an oversimplified example, consider how multiple people can listen to the same presidential candidate's impassioned speech about social welfare programs and have wildly different interpretations of what it meant and how effective it was. Some might filter the speech through dispositions of charity and empathy, others might draw upon dispositions of equity and solidarity, and still others might activate dispositions of individualism and resilience. Some might see the candidate's speaking style as inspirational. Others might see it as inflammatory. Based on one's understanding of the speech, one might decide to vote for or against the candidate, donate to the candidate's or an opponent's campaign, write a letter to the candidate supporting or refuting her or his claims, or maybe remain unchanged by what one heard. Remember too that each person harbors several dispositions, not just two as I described here. Our environments, backgrounds, identities, and prior experiences shape our dispositions, and the diversity and multiplicity of human dispositions lead to an infinite range of understandings and subsequent actions by individuals.

For the purpose of this book, we believe it's helpful to name and discuss a few dispositions that are particularly relevant to community-engaged learning, even as we hold on to the idea that several dispositions simultaneously influence a person's thoughts and actions. We'll start by exploring an unfavorable but common disposition that applies to community-engaged experiences. Then we will talk about the processes by which our dispositions can evolve or shift, especially in the context of engaged learning activities. The remainder of the chapter will describe dispositions like open-mindedness, humility, and empathy that we have found to be beneficial in shaping positive community engagement experiences for students and community.

To get you into the spirit of this chapter, as well as the next one on the responsibilities of a community-engaged learner, we invite you to watch the short video in Figure 3.1 (7 minutes) that describes how some students, faculty, and community partners conceptualize community-engaged learning and what they see as essential dispositions and behaviors for ensuring a beneficial experience.

Figure 3.1. Ready, set, engage! Principles and practice of community engagement.

Note: See video at https://vimeo.com/175587087/542059e235

Doing Time

Let's start by examining an example of a disposition that can be common among students doing community-engaged learning. It's the *doing time* mind-set. In the community-engaged course, this mentality applies specifically to the way students perceive the required commitment of hours they must fulfill outside of the classroom. At best, this disposition frames community engagement and service activities in terms of hours to be completed. At worst, it frames the service activity as a punitive imposition on students' limited free time. In other words, some students see themselves as doing time at their community partner organizations, as if they were languishing in after-school detention.

To be fair, this disposition is often fostered and reinforced by instructors who define the service activity primarily by the minimum required hours on-site at the host organization, and delineate successful completion of service as a signed hours log from the site supervisor that is turned in at the end of the semester. Further, community organizations often coordinate volunteer activities like meal service and tutoring into hourly shifts. However, even though tracking time is a common way to measure a service activity, it should not limit or exclusively define what you give or receive from that activity. To make the most of community-engaged learning, many students will likely need to engage in a dispositional shift.

How Dispositions Evolve and Shift

By definition, our dispositions can change in light of new experiences and information, but that doesn't happen often or easily. In fact, it's human nature to seek out information and experiences that align with and reinforce our worldviews. Having our worldviews confirmed by "data" from the world around us is very comforting. For example, if we agree with the common belief that people become homeless because they make bad choices like using drugs or refusing to work, we will be predisposed to notice people who are homeless and appear to be intoxicated or "lazy" (e.g., sleeping on the street, slumped over on a park bench). We will be less likely to notice people who are homeless but don't fit into our idea of what homelessness looks like or how homeless people act. We are less likely to think about the reality that, according to the U.S. Department of Housing and Urban Development (2016), 22% of the U.S. homeless population are children under the age of 18, and 31% are people over the age of 50. It's unsettling, to say the least, to dwell on thoughts of children and seniors living on the streets or in shelters, so most of us don't think about it. These realities push against the worldview that certain people choose a life of homelessness and therefore deserve it. They also challenge a common worldview that the United States, as a democratic and "civilized" country, adequately cares for its most vulnerable members, like children and seniors. Information about homeless children and seniors should alarm us and compel us to take action, but instead many of us seek comfort by shutting that information out of our minds and believing that homelessness is a conscious choice made by adults with free will but bad decision-making capacities. This allows us to think that we will always have the power to avoid homelessness as long as we make good life choices, to believe that the democratic society built by "we the people" is functioning humanely. All we have to do is work hard and make good decisions, and we'll be able to remain housed throughout our lives. Our society was built to help those who help themselves, right?

But the causes of homelessness are so much more complex than an individual's life choices. How might we come to a more nuanced understanding of, and disposition toward, the issue of homelessness and people who are unhoused? One theory suggests that our worldviews change through a process of transformative learning. The creator of this theory, Jack Mezirow, claims that transformative learning involves two important components: discourse and critical reflection.

Discourse means engaging in conversations with others for the specific purpose of examining diverse information and perspectives on a topic (Mezirow, 1997). These conversations may happen informally over dinner or coffee with friends, relatives, or even strangers. They may also be more formalized, as is the case with course-based discussions. Regardless of where and how they happen, one important caveat is that the conversations need to occur with people who have beliefs, values, and worldviews that vary from your own. We don't learn much from talking only to like-minded people all the time. Of course, discourse across diverse perspectives can often generate tension, or even conflict, but therein lies the opportunity for learning. That tension is a signal to us that our worldviews are coming up against evidence and/or assertions that what we've believed about the world throughout our lives might not be completely true. It's an uncomfortable but powerful opportunity to alter your perspective, but it doesn't happen unless you engage your mind.

Critical reflection is an internal mental process of actively interrogating our own values, beliefs, and assumptions in light of new information acquired through formal and informal education, direct experience, and discourse (Mezirow, 1997).

In essence, it involves asking ourselves hard questions, which in the case of exploring our perspectives on homelessness, might look like the following: What do I really know for a fact about homelessness? What assumptions or biases might I hold? Where did I get the information or evidence that informs my assumptions? What information is missing? What are some alternative perspectives on homelessness? Where might I find evidence that supports these alternative perspectives? How can I learn more so I can feel confident that my understanding of homelessness is well informed? In addition to digging into cognitive inquiry, you should also pay attention to the feelings that arise when you think about, talk about, observe, and interact with people who are homeless. Do you experience feelings of fear? Disdain? Guilt? Empathy? Those feelings are a function of the way you perceive homelessness. You might feel disdain if you see homelessness as a choice or guilt if you believe that our community is not living up to its responsibility to care for every community member. When you reflect on your thoughts and emotions, you can begin to identify possibilities for new learning. As we've said before, this isn't necessarily a comfortable and natural process, so it's helpful when your community-engaged course is designed to facilitate this exact kind of learning.

Key Dispositions

Although your instructor has pulled together many essential ingredients necessary to create a transformative learning experience—
academic content, community engagement activities, class discussions, reflection assignments—you will need to bring the "key"
ingredient: a set of dispositions that will allow you to turn this learning experience into a new and more informed worldview. While we
are inviting you to bring the dispositions featured in the following
sections into your community-engaged activities, we also want to
honor the idea that the community-engaged experience will develop
and hone your capacities to practice these dispositions even more
effectively. Thus, these dispositions are both an input and an outcome of high-quality community engagement.

Open-Mindedness

An open mind can lead you to amazing places. It's a disposition that
allows us to seek out new and different experiences, like traveling to
other countries or skydiving or getting a drastically different haircut.
In the context of community-engaged learning, an open mind can
help you to choose a service or engagement activity that you haven't
tried before. Maybe you served as a tutor for middle-school students
when you were in high school, but instead of choosing the tutoring
option in your community-engaged course, you choose the option
of working with the Day Laborers' Collective to advocate for local
government to implement a sanctuary city policy. Alternatively, you
might have grown up in a community affected by racialized police
brutality and organized peers to advocate for more humane and
equitable law enforcement policies. In your community-engaged
learning course, you could choose to extend the knowledge and skills
you gained from organizing in your own neighborhood to a community grappling with other youth-related issues. Whatever your
background with service and community engagement, we challenge
you to look beyond the familiar and "safe" options that replicate
your previous experiences and instead extend yourself into a new
and different situation.

Although it may feel scary to stretch outside your comfort zone, doing so allows you to learn and grow. Think about it: If you chose to do only the things that were familiar and safe, you probably never would have learned how to ride a bike or navigate around the city on a public bus or come to college. And each of these examples illustrates a transformative experience in a person's young life. Consider the sense of freedom you achieved when you could ride your bike down the street without training wheels or an adult pushing you along. Think about how public transportation allows you to explore the diverse offerings of your community. Reflect on the way college has fostered a sense of independence and autonomy that prepares you for the growing responsibilities of adulthood. Of course, when you learned to ride your bike, you probably fell or crashed a few times. And we're guessing that, as you learned to navigate the bus system, you may have found yourself on a bus route that was unfamiliar and took you in a different direction than intended. And there have probably been some times in college when you've felt overwhelmed by the responsibilities of juggling school, work, social life, and other commitments. But just because these experiences haven't all been easy and positive doesn't mean they haven't been worth it.

The same holds true for your community-engaged learning experience. It's meant to push you out of the comfort zone of your campus classroom and into a vibrant community where residents struggle, thrive, and grapple with issues of injustice and marginalization. In your community-engaged course, you will likely have the opportunity to develop and practice new skills, form new relationships, develop knowledge about a particular community, and analyze social justice issues through direct engagement with them. This experience can be positive if you enter into it with, and maintain, an open mind. What does this look like in practice? Well, to start, you need to be open to listening to the narratives of the people you are interacting with in the community. What you may find is that people live and think differently than you, and that their worldviews are rooted in their life experiences. They will likely share perspectives you've never considered or stories that challenge the way you think the world works. Your initial reaction may be to shut down or dismiss information that doesn't align with your existing understandings, so you should counter that by proactively listening and reflecting on the meaning of people's stories. You should be open to the possibility that interactions and discourse with other people could change the way you think about an issue or a group.

In addition to being open to different kinds of community-engaged activities and practicing openness as you engage others in dialogue and listen to their perspectives, it's also important to welcome the learning and growth that come from failure and feedback. Not all of our community-engaged learning experiences are going to run smoothly. You might find yourself in a situation that requires you to deploy skills that you haven't yet mastered or negotiate a challenging interaction without feeling equipped to do so. You might say or do something that triggers anger, fear, or pain in another person. You might complete a project in a way that doesn't meet the expectations of your community partner. Alternatively, you may discover that the failure was prompted by circumstances beyond your control. Perhaps there was staff turnover at your partner organization, or they lost funding for the project you were working on, or they had to reprioritize their focus in response to a policy shift. Each of these situations could cause your project to be altered or even terminated. We hope these challenges don't happen to you, but if they do, it is another chance for you to harvest some learning. Spend some time reflecting on the situation. What caused this to happen? Who was involved in creating the situation and who is responsible for making it right? What can I personally do to demonstrate accountability and commitment to the project? In response to this last question, seek and invite feedback from your community partner, peers, and instructor. Listen to what they say and try to avoid getting defensive or placing blame. Recognize that, even when we have the best of intentions, we can make mistakes or fall short of other people's expectations. Of course, when mistakes or challenges arise, if we have the capacity, we should rectify them. If the situation is beyond repair, commit to allowing this failure or challenge to inform the way you act in the future. This indicates an open mind and demonstrates a disposition of humility.

Humility

Whereas open-mindedness may prompt you to tackle new adventures and challenges, humility is the force that will help you recognize and honor your own limitations. Just like other dispositions, humility and its opposite, arrogance, are learned primarily through informal education. As children, we observe how adults behave and mimic their actions. As youth and young adults, we may model our behaviors after peers or public figures: political leaders, singers, actors, professional athletes. Some of us may also learn about humility more formally or intentionally through our faith traditions. Examples of humility and arrogance play out in our lives daily.

In fact, there's a term for the arrogant mind-set that our dominant culture fosters in us with regard to community service. It's called the *savior (industrial) complex*, and it means that many of us have been socialized to believe in the narrative that a single person can drop into an unjust situation for a brief period and "save the day" like a superhero. Specifically, if we think about the story arcs for almost all of the popular superheroes—Superman, Batman, Spiderman—they involve the hero independently vanquishing the bad guys. The hero acts alone, often succeeding by working outside of the law and operating literally and figuratively above the community he aims to protect. He flies, climbs, or swings from skyscrapers, causing all sorts of mayhem on the streets as he chases down the bad guys at any cost. And these hero stories never show the collateral damage of the hero's single-minded desire to save the day, but we can imagine what it might look like: overturned cars and broken windows, people caught in the crossfire of a shootout or maimed in crashes during the chase scene. We know this is all fictitious destruction, but how might we use it as a metaphor for the potential impact of our desire to be heroes or saviors of the community? What collateral damage might we create when we drop in with good intentions but too much arrogance and attempt to "fix" or "help" a community grappling with injustice? It won't be as dramatic as the destruction we see in blockbuster superhero movies, but real harm can be done if we are not careful.

If that example was a little too dramatic for you, let's look at a more realistic scenario: After taking a sociology class on inequities in the education system, college students decide to start a tutoring program for youth in the working-class neighborhood adjacent to their campus. They plan to invite middle-school students to a designated study lounge on campus twice a week to help them with homework, but they quickly grow frustrated with how the youth are responding to this opportunity. At the outset, it's hard to get more than a few middle schoolers to agree to participate, even after outreach efforts that included posting signs around the community and e-mailing the neighborhood public schools. The youth who agree to participate don't show up consistently, and when they do, they are resistant to the tutors' instruction. The tutors manifest their frustration by questioning whether the middle schoolers really do want to succeed, which prompts the youth to feel discouraged, unsafe, and unsupported. After only a few weeks, the college students give up on the program because no more youth are showing up. They chalk up the failure as an indicator that families in the adjacent community don't care about their kids' education.

It is often the case that idealistic individuals from privileged backgrounds will become aware of injustices, like unequal access to education, and feel compelled to act, perhaps by starting a small-scale charity effort or even a nonprofit organization. These idealists may be motivated by a sense of compassion, outrage, and/or duty. Their efforts may be informed by analysis of statistics, expert scholarship, government reports, and other published data sources. Although there is passion and research behind these interventions, there is also arrogance when privileged idealists aspire to be heroes to those who are oppressed. The implicit assumption is that the idealist's own will and intellect are sufficient foundations for effective social change interventions.

In the case of the tutoring program, if the students had come from a place of humility, they might have realized the need to ask more questions. What are the particular opportunity gaps and academic challenges in this community? Who would have the best insight about what these challenges are? What tutoring programs and other educational interventions already exist in the community?

In what ways are these existing interventions successful or struggling? What learning interventions and supports are most responsive to the particular values, challenges, and needs of youth in this community? What motivates youth to participate in tutoring? What training, background, and qualifications does one need to effectively support youth learning in a one-on-one or small-group setting? As they found answers to these questions, they probably would have discovered that their current knowledge and skills were not sufficient to take the lead on implementing an intervention at this time, in this particular community.

We can't completely blame the students for their missteps. We are conditioned into the savior complex in a number of ways, including how our history books convey oversimplified stories of transformative historical social movements. As a society, we celebrate iconic leaders like Dr. Martin Luther King Jr., Harvey Milk, or Cesar Chavez for catalyzing significant shifts toward a more just and equitable society. Their dedication, strategic leadership, and personal sacrifice were essential to fostering major civil and human rights victories. And yet they did not win these battles alone. There were many people who contributed their own capacities, gifts, and commitments as foot soldiers in the movements. How often are we invited to honor and emulate the thousands of other activists who humbly dedicated themselves to the arduous and dangerous work of mobilizing to advance iconic leaders' visions of social justice? What might we gain by including acknowledgment of the foot soldiers in our historical narratives even as we continue to celebrate the heroism of movement leaders? Might this create space for each of us to imagine a role in social change that allows us to humbly reflect on our strengths and limitations and then leverage our unique capacities in support of movements? Might this be a way to release us from the dominant cultural expectation that we must always be the hero while still holding us accountable for contributing to positive change?

Given these considerations, how can we make sure that we are not trying to replicate these savior narratives in the way we do community-engaged learning? How can we recognize our limitations as students, young people, and/or outsiders to the community?

How can we be of use in a way that demonstrates humility but also generates a positive impact?

To start, we can see community-engaged learning as an opportunity to build our understandings and capacities by tapping into the collective wisdom and strength of community members. We exhibit humility by recognizing the value of others' strengths and resources. As you go into community, you can look to the residents, service providers, and community leaders to show you how this application of humility looks in action. You are likely to observe community leaders working collaboratively with residents to accomplish goals, rather than trying to change things on their own. You are likely to see service providers asking clients about their priorities and needs for the purpose of shaping social services to be more responsive. You are likely to see youth teaching their elders how to speak English or use a computer, which requires the elders to take up the role of student instead of teacher. You are likely to have conversations with people in recovery from addiction, who speak about their journey to sobriety, employment, and peace in ways that foster new insights about addiction that cannot be gleaned from statistical reports and clinical studies. And your job will be to act as an apprentice to these humble agents of change in your community—seeking their wisdom, emulating their actions, and contributing to their change efforts.

In addition to drawing upon community members as resources, we must also recognize that all communities, even those struggling with injustice, are filled with assets. Examples of these assets include schools, businesses, and service organizations. They include gathering spaces like parks and community centers. They include informal associations like book clubs or neighborhood watch groups. And most importantly, they include people who have their own unique wisdom, skills, and talents to share with others. Communities don't need external heroes to save them. Marginalized communities have all the ingredients to create their own change, even as they struggle against systems and legacies of oppression that have been created to keep them from thriving. The way we can fit into their social change work is by apprenticing ourselves to the people who are leading the change.

To be an apprentice means to learn a cohesive set of competencies from a seasoned expert in the field while also applying emerging skills and knowledge in support of the expert's work. It requires us to first acknowledge that there are things we don't know and must learn from those with experience. We must also recognize that wisdom and expertise are not solely located within the walls of academia or within the minds of our instructors. Rather, every person accumulates these things through life experiences, as well as formal and informal educational processes. We can and do learn some of the most valuable lessons about the world and ourselves through observation, discourse, and interaction with diverse others, whose identities and experiences range in terms of socioeconomic status, ethnicity, gender, educational attainment, and ability, to name a few. How can you create space in your mind and heart to learn from the community leaders and community members around you?

Further, just as we practice humility in the way we position ourselves as learners, we must also infuse humility into the tasks, activities, and responsibilities that comprise the community-engaged experience. We have to be willing to take up the tasks that are most pressing in the work of our host organizations and community, whether they seem complicated or mundane. For example, you might be asked to knock on the doors of local residents to conduct a survey about community safety, which can be daunting if you're introverted or unfamiliar with the neighborhood. Reflection will help you identify and name this limitation, and open-mindedness will help you move through it. Or maybe your host organization really needs you to input data from temporary housing applications into their shared database. This might seem really tedious, especially if you aren't sure how this task connects to the mission and services of the organization. It's helpful, in these instances, to consider how your particular tasks or projects integrate into the larger vision and mission of the organization. If you're struggling to make the connection, ask your supervisor to help you understand the "big picture" and your place in it. Humility will help you trust that your community partner is making the best use of your presence, and open-mindedness will guide you to derive learning from the experience.

We must share one more important note about humility in the context of cross-cultural interactions. Many, but not all, community-engaged learning activities involve students with identity groups different from their own. You may find yourself connecting to groups that are familiar or unfamiliar to you, but regardless of your level of familiarity, there's a need to espouse a culturally humble approach to engagement. Melanie Tervalon and Jann Murray-Garcia (1998) coined the term *cultural humility* to describe an aspirational disposition they felt should be infused into healthcare delivery. Cultural humility means honoring the diversity of values, beliefs, experiences, and traditions that make up various cultures by learning from direct interactions with culturally diverse people while also recognizing the inherent limitations of our capacities to understand and operate within cultures that are not our own. Those who practice cultural humility recognize that they will never achieve an "end goal" of cultural competence, but rather they will engage in a lifelong process of learning and growth with regard to appreciating and valuing the cultural experiences of others.

Appreciation of Community Cultural Wealth

For the purpose of enacting cultural humility in your community-engaged learning course, one effective framework is community cultural wealth (Yosso, 2005). Community cultural wealth describes a collection of assets that are specifically fostered in, and deployed by, communities of color as they engage in collective and individual struggles to thrive within oppressive systems. Yosso categorizes these assets as aspirational, linguistic, familial, social, navigational, and resistance.

Aspirational wealth is summarized as persistent hope in the face of adversity. In action, this looks like people responding to community challenges in ways that make them collectively and individually stronger. For example, the community may respond to a police shooting of an unarmed teenager by holding peace vigils and advocating for a change to use-of-force policies. Similarly, aspirational wealth is portrayed in public murals depicting the diversity of modern community life or in the spirituals sung by enslaved people to convey their aspirations toward freedom. As you engage community members, where do you see examples of their manifestations of hope? What are some symbols, spaces, and events that demonstrate and perpetuate the community's hopes and dreams?

As you'd expect, linguistic wealth recognizes that fluency in other languages besides English is a powerful and useful skill. Linguistic wealth also encompasses the specific ways communities of color communicate their culture within and beyond their identity group, including storytelling, poetry, music, and so on. What languages are spoken by people in the community in which you are engaging? Who is using these languages and who isn't? Are the languages of the community reflected in the local signage? What stories are shared with you by community members? What are the underlying messages or themes in these stories? In what ways do you see the community using stories, poetry, and music to create unity? In what ways do you see the community using stories, poetry, and/or music to educate others who are not part of their culture?

Familial and social capital refer to the need for individuals to rely upon the connections they build with family members, peers, and mentors internal to the community. This grows out of the value that many communities of color place on interdependence. Through connection with others, one becomes stronger. What social activities are taking place in the community? How do people greet each other across generations or cultures? Where do you see evidence of interdependence playing out?

Navigational capital describes the capacity to maneuver through social and civic institutions and spaces that were not built to include communities of color in equitable ways. Who accesses various spaces in the community (think in terms of demographics)? How do community members interact with public officials or public servants in venues like town halls, schools, or parks? How do people talk about educational, law enforcement, and social service institutions? Where do you see evidence of people adapting to "fit into" different environments?

Finally, community cultural wealth encompasses resistance capital, which is the learned legacy of struggle that many people of color feel compelled to carry forward. Youth internalize this capital by observing their family, community members, local leaders, and historical figures, and then they adapt it to their particular historical, geographic, and social contexts. Thus, social movements evolve to address the ever-changing systems of oppression of each new era. Community members deploy resistance capital in overt and subtle ways as they not only navigate but also actively work to transform oppressive systems. We encourage you to learn about the various ways people perform resistance so you can develop understanding and empathy for their efforts. Are there institutions or informal associations in the community that frame their work in terms of resistance, social transformation, or social justice? What actions or activities do these groups take? Who are the voices for change in the community? To whom are those voices speaking? What are the messages of resistance coming from community (grassroots) institutions, leaders, and residents?

Intellectual Curiosity

The preceding questions not only demonstrate a posture of cultural humility but also illustrate intellectual curiosity, another essential disposition for community-engaged learners. In fact, intellectual curiosity is an extension of open-mindedness and humility. We can progress from having the humility to know that there's always more we must learn to marshalling the will to learn new things to asking complex questions about how the world works and seeking answers. Intellectual curiosity also spurs us to analyze and synthesize evidence gained through our experiences to formulate new understandings about the systems and structures that govern our world.

Unfortunately, traditional educational practices often serve to stifle students' curiosity. Starting in kindergarten, many children are taught that the purpose of education is to learn the prescribed answers to pre-existing questions: What is a quadrilateral? When did Abraham Lincoln become president? Who wrote *Charlotte's Web*? In most classrooms, the teacher is positioned as the expert who supplies all the academic questions and answers, whereas the student is positioned as the receiver of the teacher's prepackaged questions and answers. Few children have access to education that allows them to define pertinent questions and undergo a process of answering them in ways that leverage both collective wisdom and individual curiosity and creativity. More often, students are subjected to exams, worksheets, drills, lectures, and textbooks, all of which aim to either provide or solicit predetermined information.

Thus, when you come into community-engaged courses, you may feel uncomfortable with the opportunity to shape and define your own learning. In fact, your initial inclination may be to seek detailed directions from your instructor about what you are supposed to do and learn while you are in the classroom and community. You may be operating under the (mis)conception that there is only one right way to do community engagement or only one right answer to the big questions that frame your community-engaged course. If you hold on to this misconception as you move through the course, you will miss a lot of potentially valuable learning about yourself, the community, and social justice issues.

Instead of focusing on "doing it right" or "getting the right answer," let's start from a disposition of intellectual curiosity (or even intellectual freedom!). Consider what you want to learn from this experience. Do you want to improve your verbal communication skills? Do you want to learn how motivation theories play out in real-world workplaces? Do you want to figure out whether a nonprofit job is right for you? Do you want to gain a better understanding of food insecurity? Let your own desires and questions shape the way you enter into your community-engaged learning, but be prepared for the reality that all your questions may not be answered by the end of the course. In fact, you may leave with more questions than answers, and that's a good thing.

For now, let's stick with this thrilling possibility that you can define your own big questions and desired outcomes in regard to community engagement. Take some time to write down some big questions that seem relevant and appropriate to what your community-engaged course entails. Again, if you need a little bit of structure to support your thinking, you might organize your questions into categories like self, community, and social issues. For each question you generate, think about what information and/or experiences might provide the building blocks to help you answer it. For example, if your question is about how to improve communication skills through community-engaged learning, you might want to focus on observing strong communicators, engaging in conversations with individuals, and/or presenting to small groups in the community setting. Perhaps you will also commit to contributing a few comments to each in-class discussion and being the lead presenter for your group presentation. As you accumulate these experiences, your intellectual curiosity should also push you to new understandings. By reflecting on your experiences, you may come to realize that you find it easier to communicate your ideas to individuals instead of groups. You may find that asking people questions about themselves and offering information about yourself is a good foundation upon which to dialogue about challenging topics. You may find that people who demonstrate strong communication skills are also very knowledgeable about the topics they choose. Each of these realizations, emerging from your own intellectual curiosity, can serve to make you a better communicator in the future.

Now let's look at another question, one that's more knowledge-based instead of skill-based. If you wanted to learn about food insecurity, how might that inform the way you move through your community-engaged course (assuming food insecurity is a relevant topic to the course content)? Hopefully, your instructor would provide you with articles and statistics on the topic, but you may find that those articles generate more questions than answers, so you might do some independent research online or at the library. You might also seek out perspectives and narratives about food insecurity through direct dialogue with community members, documentaries, memoirs, or blogs. You might schedule a meeting with your community partner to ask questions about how the organization addresses food insecurity, how public policy affects food access, and how government assistance programs work. Based on analysis of these accumulated data, you may come to find that food insecurity intersects with other social justice issues like homelessness, poverty, and health disparities. You might notice that government assistance provides some help to people who cannot afford to buy adequate amounts of food, but it isn't enough to ensure that a person gets three healthy and nutritious meals a day. You may come to realize that transportation, geography, physical ability, and language all function to facilitate or hinder access to food. Learning these things through your community-engaged course will make you a more informed and (hopefully) empathetic community member. Again, this is an example of learning that extends beyond the course or the final exam. This is learning that affects who you are, how you see the world, and how you act.

Now imagine a parallel universe in which you didn't employ intellectual curiosity in your community-engaged course. Instead, you moved through the community activities like you were "doing time" or as if you had blinders on. Your single-minded focus was to complete the course, get a passing grade, and move on to the next academic term in your slow march toward a college degree. You moved through the community with your shoulders hunched, eyes downcast, and headphones over your ears. You avoided the attempts of others to engage you in conversation. You completed tasks as quickly as possible and then hastened back to campus or hid in a corner while you gazed at your phone screen to minimize the possibility that you would be invited to take up a new task or activity. At the end of the term, what do you think you would have learned in this scenario? Our guess is that you probably learned very little, which makes the experience a huge waste of everyone's time.

As you can see, intellectual curiosity is a disposition that will serve you well not only in your community-engaged course but also in life. Think of yourself as a sponge ready to absorb as much new information as possible. As you move from campus into community, *observe* what is around you. Where are the community assets? Who is present in various community spaces and who is missing? Who interacts and how? What visual messaging is being communicated by businesses, government, and organizations through signs, art, and architecture? What sounds do you hear as you move through the community—music, laughter, shouting, traffic—and what do they tell you about how the community functions? *Interact* with people respectfully, humbly, and curiously. Who can you talk to and what will you ask them? What is each person's story? What do they care about? What does each person know that you don't yet know? What things do you have in common? What are your differences and what is the root of those differences? What can you learn from each other? *Research* what you can't discover through direct experience. What do scholars and practitioners have to say on this topic? How does the news media present this issue? What sources can you find that draw upon narratives and experiences of marginalized people? How can statistics help you understand the scope of the issue? *Reflect* on the accumulated data and experiences to synthesize new understandings about our world. Which evidence reinforces your current point of view and which evidence challenges it? What connections or discrepancies do you see across your experiences and other data sources? What might explain the discrepancies? What have you learned about yourself, the community, and social issues from the community-engaged learning experience? What big questions will you continue to grapple with?

Intellectual curiosity is an essential disposition to fuel lifelong learning, but given that we necessarily learn from interaction with other humans, we are ethically bound to couple this curiosity with a disposition of empathy.

Empathy

Although we are encouraging you to learn from people in community, we are not advocating for you to interrogate them like a detective or a lawyer. Being on the receiving end of a rapid-fire series of questions about one's life experience is not a comfortable situation. That's why it's so important to exercise empathy, not just in your conversations but also in the way you interact with and think about others. For the purposes of this book, let's stick with the dictionary definition of *empathy*:

> The action of understanding, being aware of, being sensitive to, and vicariously experiencing the feelings, thoughts, and experience of another . . . without having the feelings, thoughts, and experience fully communicated in an objectively explicit manner. (Merriam-Webster, 2017)

What we like about this definition is that it names sensitivity as an essential ingredient of empathy. It's possible to be aware of the feelings and experiences of others but not be sensitive to them, but that is a callous way to engage our human family. Instead, we should attempt to imagine how we would feel if we were in that person's situation while also maintaining (cultural) humility, meaning we continue to carry recognition of our own limitations with regard to truly being able to replicate within ourselves the feelings experienced by another person. This is especially true when we are attempting to empathize with people who have experienced marginalization or oppression in the ways that we experience privilege. Think about it: If you've never been the target of domestic violence, you can attempt to imagine the terror and powerlessness that a person might feel in that situation, but you will never know the depth of the impact that sort of experience has if it hasn't happened directly to you. Similarly, if you've never had to pick strawberries for 12 hours a day in the California summer heat, you might be able to guess at how such labor would affect one's body and mind, but you won't truly understand the implications of how that work shapes the person who is doing it unless you've done the same work. Although we can never fully understand and feel the impact of another's situation unless we've experienced it directly ourselves, we have a responsibility to strive for an approximate understanding and demonstrate the requisite sensitivity as we learn more about the human experience.

Another important component of the *empathy* definition is that one should be able to demonstrate understanding and sensitivity toward other persons without them having to describe their experience in copious detail in order to motivate empathy. To be clear, shared narratives are powerful vehicles for building empathy, but most people don't feel comfortable divulging intimate details of their life stories to strangers. If you haven't been a consistent presence in the community before your instructor required it, then it's likely you'll first be met with wariness and suspicion until you prove that you are worthy of trust. Thus, your first efforts to learn about and empathize with community members will probably grow out of observations and informal interactions. In many cases, you will likely be able to read the physical manifestations of people's feelings by noticing how their bodies move, how they do and don't connect with each other verbally and physically, how they inhabit or avoid certain spaces, and how they dress and carry themselves. We must draw an important distinction here between being an observant participant in community life and observing others in a voyeuristic way from a distance. There are many valid and important critiques of community engagement as "poverty tourism," and that is not the model we are condoning. Rather, we are encouraging you to find a balance between curiosity and empathy as you engage in authentic interactions with people in the community. And just as you notice the behaviors of people around you and attempt to extrapolate an understanding of what they are feeling, you should do the same sort of reflection on your own actions and feelings as they emerge in response to the community context.

For some of us, empathy seems to come naturally. As we see other people experiencing joy, we can't help but feel joyful ourselves. When we see a person suffering, we are moved by empathy to act in ways that attempt to alleviate the pain for them. For others, empathy comes less easily, but we can actively cultivate it, just like other dispositions. Consider some of the following questions as you build empathy through engaging with diverse community members: What emotions and feelings do I interpret from the verbal and physical cues of another person? What are my own reactions to this person and where are they coming from? What do I know about this person's situation? What am I assuming based on the context? What have people directly shared with me? Have I had similar experiences that I can draw upon to help me empathize with them? If so, in what ways are our experiences similar and different? If not, how might my limited understanding bias my analysis of their feelings and actions? Assuming I want to grow my capacity to empathize with others, what can I do to learn more about diverse life experiences? Of course, this brings us back to that disposition of intellectual curiosity because learning to empathize means gathering and reflecting on new information about people. As mentioned in the previous section, this is most effectively done through direct interaction, dialogue, and seeking diverse narratives in print and media. It's possible that extending your learning in this way might not be an expectation that your instructor has articulated in the syllabus, so it may require your own willingness to commit to developing this disposition.

Commitment

Think about the people to whom you've felt committed over the span of your life. Many of us feel a strong commitment to our family members, and we show it by spending time with them, tending to their needs, acting in ways that please them, and offering gestures of affection. It is a sense of commitment that leads us to prioritize family, even though we juggle competing demands on our time and attention, and persevere through conflict to maintain familial relationships. In other words, interpersonal commitments (familial and otherwise) are an essential condition of authentic relationships. Although the people to whom we are committed may change over time, when we feel a commitment to someone, we show up for them.

Commitment also applies to activities. If you've ever played a competitive sport, you'll know that it requires a great deal of dedication. Athletes must put time, physical energy, and mental effort into building their skills and strength, learning how the game is played and the strategies to win, and engaging in healthy eating and sleeping behaviors. Commitment means showing up to early morning practice when you would rather sleep in and forgoing greasy pizza in favor of lean protein and vegetables for your pregame meal. In other words, being a competitive athlete requires one to feel responsibility to something larger than one's self—the team. Thus, the athlete makes choices that prioritize the team's success.

Community-engaged learning requires a disposition of commitment. In the next chapter, we get specific about how you will demonstrate this through your actions, but for now we are just going to make the case for why commitment matters to community engagement. We emphasize the primary barrier to commitment—*time*—so you can be proactive about addressing it.

Commitment is crucial to community engagement because many courses require students to directly engage with organizations that serve marginalized and vulnerable groups. To be marginalized and vulnerable means that one's capacity to affect changes in one's own life is extremely limited because of institutional systems and structures of oppression. If you've already activated a disposition of empathy for individuals experiencing marginalization and oppression, that's a good starting point for understanding why commitment is essential in the community context.

If your host organization serves people who claim one or multiple marginalized identities, it probably has established practices, protocols, and procedures to create safe spaces for people to access support, services, and/or solidarity. Staff at the organization have likely invested in building mutually trusting relationships with those who rely on the organization. You, as an outsider, a new presence at the site, and a (temporary) representative of your host organization, must be willing to commit to upholding the practices, protocols and procedures, as well as embodying the vision, culture, and values of the organization while you are affiliated with it. If you don't, there's a possibility of damaging the organization's relationships with its constituents or causing harm in other ways. In sum, the organization is taking a risk by inviting you to join in their work, so you must commit to putting the good of the organization and its constituents above other priorities while you are in your community-engaged course.

Hopefully, your commitment to your host organization is organic, reflecting a predisposition to care about the issues that are being addressed and the people being served. In the best case, the host organization's mission and values resonate with your own, and the organization's work aligns with your interests, so you can easily commit to contributing to their work. But we won't kid ourselves that this is always the case. You might find that you'll be working with an organization addressing issues that (at least initially) you care very little about. Nevertheless, it is essential that you commit to supporting their work with integrity, which means learning not only what they do but why, how, and for whom. In rare cases, students may find that the values and culture of the organization are so divergent from their own that they can't morally or ethically commit to advancing the organization's work. If you experience this, it is a valid issue to discuss with your instructor.

Of course, students' ability to commit to their community organization is usually affected by much less dramatic (and much more mundane) barriers than conflicting values. The biggest challenge arises for students who are overextended with too many simultaneous commitments. We recognize that many students are taking full course loads, working or interning part time, and balancing social lives and family obligations. That is a lot to juggle, and it can be difficult to figure out what to prioritize when everything seems important. The time that your course requires you to be in the community could seem like an extra burden on top of all these things, but for your host organization, your regular and reliable presence is essential for them to be able to provide services. Further, your time in community is a valuable opportunity to learn and grow while also contributing positively to something bigger than yourself. And once you embrace the opportunity, you need to proactively problem-solve any time-related barriers that emerge. How can you make space for community engagement in your schedule such that you honor the gravity of your commitment to an organization that works with and for marginalized people? Are there creative ways that you can work with the organization that allow for scheduling flexibility? Are there other commitments that you can put on hold and pick up again after your course culminates? Are there friends, family, or colleagues who can temporarily take on some of your ongoing responsibilities?

Making space for community-engaged learning in your schedule may not be easy, but it will be worthwhile. Just remember, as we've said before, community engagement is not just about doing time; it's also about actively contributing to community change, so let's talk about the responsibilities that come with being an aspiring change agent.

4

RESPONSIBILITIES

What We Need to Do as Community-Engaged Learners

We have spent a lot of time describing dispositions that will allow you to enter into community-engaged learning ready to succeed, but it's essential to translate these dispositions into action. This chapter will provide practical advice for how to meet the responsibilities inherent in community-engaged learning, regardless of where your engagement takes place.

We begin by emphasizing the importance of making human connections and building relationships. Community engagement is about interacting with others in ways that are mutually beneficial. It's not just about your learning process, and it's not just about getting a grade. Thus, you should resist the urge to focus solely on the outcome, output, or final product of this course. Although it is important to accomplish the mutually determined outcomes of your community-engaged course, the *way* you achieve those outcomes is just as important as *whether* you achieve them. We invite you to embrace the responsibility to act in ways that build mutual trust and respect, and we'll share some ideas about how to do so.

Next, we provide an overview of professional behavior. Enacting professionalism is a crucial responsibility because your presence at your host organization means you represent its values and vision to community constituents and clients. Your actions should reflect congruence with the organizational culture. Similarly, working at an organization necessarily means that you should conform to the policies and practices that govern how the organization functions.

One important aspect of both professionalism and building relationships is communication. Although it intersects with these other responsibilities, we've made it a separate section in this chapter to illuminate its importance. Indeed, the majority of issues that arise in community-engaged learning are the result of miscommunication or lack of communication. Many constituents are involved in your community-engaged experience, and each has his or her own expectations, capacities, worldviews, and needs. These are the filters through which they (and you) give and receive information, creating a high likelihood of miscommunication. How can you communicate consistently and effectively to reduce the possibility of problems arising? We'll tell you in a bit! For now, just recognize that you are responsible for communicating openly, honestly, and proactively with your peers, site supervisor, community members, and instructor to reduce the potential for harmful communication errors and increase the opportunities for project success.

We will also demystify the act of reflection. Contrary to popular belief, reflection in the context of community-engaged learning is not about generating and sharing warm fuzzy feelings about our efforts to serve others. Rather, reflection is the process of making meaning of experiences by integrating our intellectual, emotional, and spiritual responses to them. It's the enactment of intellectual curiosity and open-mindedness, tempered by humility and infused with empathy. It's a complex but valuable process that enhances skills useful not just in community-engaged courses but also in your everyday life. It may seem odd to label this as a responsibility, but practicing reflection is crucial to processing your community-engaged experience in a way that generates new learning and understanding. You have a responsibility to yourself, your instructor, and your site supervisor to engage fully in every component of the community-engaged course, including the various formal and informal reflection opportunities.

Taken in sum, this may seem like a lot of responsibility compared to a typical academic course, but that's because community-engaged learning has higher stakes. As we mentioned in the previous chapter, there's potential to do harm, even if we don't intend to. The practical advice in this chapter is our attempt to minimize the possibility of inadvertently doing harm and maximize the mutual benefits.

Making Human Connections

Let's start with your most important responsibility—connecting with other people. The term *engage* conveys an explicit expectation that you interact with the people around you. To engage others requires that you talk to them, ask questions and answer theirs, listen to their perspectives, and display body language and facial expressions that are open and welcoming. Making human connections through words and actions is about building trust, demonstrating respect, and honoring people's dignity and humanity. And although these values may seem optional in the context of providing service to others, we argue that they are integral. Think about it: When you're in a bind, whom do you call? A family member? A friend? Your favorite high school teacher? Many of us have the luxury of choosing whom we ask to help us through challenging times. We're guessing you call upon people you know and trust to provide support without passing judgment or taking advantage of your vulnerability. However, there are a number of people who are unable to rely solely upon friends and family as their safety net. Instead, they must count on support provided through human services agencies and nonprofit organizations. Because these organizations rely on volunteers to deliver services, it's likely that people accessing these services are receiving them from strangers. We imagine that this might trigger feelings like resignation, resentment, suspicion, and distrust for some recipients, just as much as it elicits optimism, gratitude, and trust in others. Although we aren't in a position to change the circumstances of how (and from whom) people access support and services, we can be mindful of our individual responsibility to engender trust and demonstrate respect.

To that end, think about engagement as falling along a continuum of *thin* to *thick*. Think of thin engagement as the bare minimum of interaction. This might entail limiting verbal communication to service transactions (e.g., telling the student you are tutoring whether she got the correct answer on her math homework or asking the person in line at the soup kitchen if he wants a roll with his stew). It may manifest as relying on physical barriers in community spaces to ensure segregation from residents or people accessing services (e.g., staying in the administrative office instead of going into the space where the clients are). It probably manifests as avoiding opportunities to socialize with the organization's staff, volunteers, and clients during lunch breaks or after service shifts. In other words, thin engagement can send a message that you don't really want to be there and community-engaged learning is just a chore to be done. Even if the root of your thin engagement is shyness or awkwardness in social settings, it can still be perceived negatively by others. It is highly likely that this behavior will beget similar responses from the people around you. People will respond to your thin engagement with their own dispassion and disconnection. This will not be an enjoyable way to move through your community-engaged course.

Alternatively, you could strive to engage thickly with people in the community. For starters, you could make an effort to greet people both as you make your way to your host site and while you are there. If you're entering a community whose primary language is different from your own, why not learn basic greeting phrases and use them? Beyond the initial exchange of pleasantries, look for opportunities to ask people questions about themselves. Stick with questions that aren't too personal, like asking someone about their favorite food at the soup kitchen or asking a child about her favorite subject in school. You don't want to come across as an interrogator, so feel free to offer information about yourself too. On the one hand, the mutual exchange of (nonsensitive) information is a way of building trust and understanding. It demonstrates care and empathy. On the other hand, it's also important to set boundaries and make sure you aren't developing a level of intimacy that could feel unsafe to others or you. As specific relationships flourish, you may find people sharing details about their lives that give insight into their realities. You should receive this information with an open mind and without judgment. This is an opportunity to reflect on the diversity of life experiences that shape people's worldviews.

The good thing is that when you choose to engage thickly with the people around you, they tend to reciprocate. You may feel affirmed in your own humanity through the verbal, physical, and social connections you nurture in community. In addition to cultivating relationships and enjoying the warm feelings that grow out of connecting with others, remember that this is still meant to be a learning experience in which you provide a value-added service to a host organization, so professionalism is essential as well.

Professional Behavior

We know it's a cliché, but we just have to say it: The first step in acting professionally is showing up—on time and ready to be of use. One of the most common complaints among community partners is that students show up late and appear tired and disengaged when they arrive (Blouin & Perry, 2009; Cronley, Madden, & Davis, 2015; Sandy, 2007). How does this do harm? Perhaps the organization is depending on you to support their service delivery, and if you arrive late, they have to muddle through shorthanded. Or maybe your site supervisor has set aside a brief window of time in her busy day to provide instructions about the project she expects you to complete, but if you arrive late and miss the scheduled check-in, you set the project back. And we already mentioned in the previous chapter how your mood and disposition can be interpreted by staff, volunteers, and community members. Showing up late can make you seem disengaged, even if that's not what you mean to convey.

So what should you do? Plan your route to and from your community site before your first day. Note bus schedules, bike routes, parking garages, and so on so you can allow enough time to get from campus (or home) to the organization. Allow extra time for your first few trips to the site, until you get a solid sense of how long it actually takes to get there. If something arises that causes you to be late or have to miss a community visit, notify your supervisor and instructor as soon as possible. Use multiple modes of communication so you can be sure that your supervisor gets the message. To the extent possible, you should expect to make up missed time by staying later or scheduling time on another day. This demonstrates dedication and responsibility.

Typically, your host site will offer an orientation of some sort to convey rules, policies, and performance expectations. It's a good idea to make notes during the orientation to help you remember all the useful information that is shared. It's likely that your site supervisor will cover check-in and check-out procedures, expectations for appropriate dress, access to particular spaces and resources, policies about how to interact with clients and community, and protocols for dealing with emergency situations. If the supervisor doesn't cover something that's on your mind, ask about it! For instance, it's probably helpful to ask about policies related to cell phone use, language use (e.g., no foul language at youth organizations), eating on-site, and so on. Note that many organizations require students to sign volunteer agreements and other paperwork, like liability waivers, either in an orientation or on the first day at the host site. Be prepared for this step in your onboarding process.

If your organization does not offer an orientation, you should proactively reach out to your site supervisor to discuss these matters and/or request that this information be shared with you electronically or in hard copy. Also, you may not know what rules and information you need until you're well into your commitment at the organization. Don't be afraid to keep asking questions about how things are done, even if you have already been there for weeks or months. It's better to be informed than to guess at the organization's rules and regulations. In this way, you can be sure that your actions align with the professional expectations of your host site.

In fact, why not take your efforts one step further? Try researching the mission, values, and services provided by your host organization. Again, this may be covered in an orientation, but you can also find this information on the organization's website or in print materials. Analyzing its mission, vision, and values will help you to understand the organization's approach to making positive community change and determine the extent to which their work aligns with your own worldview. As with the rules and regulations, it's a good idea to discuss the organization's vision, mission, and values with your site supervisor, who might be able to provide background or contextual information about how the organization's work is shaped by these ideals. Further, you should observe for yourself how the organization turns its ideals into action in day-to-day services. Notice how services and vision seem to be congruent or incongruent, and bring those observations into the classroom for reflection with peers. Depending on the nature of your relationship with your site supervisor, you might also be able to share your observations and get her or his insights on what you noticed. You can learn so much about organizational culture and how social justice issues are challenged or reinforced just from observing how the organization runs.

However, remember that you're not going into community just to observe and analyze what you see. If your community-engaged course requires you to complete a project, it's your responsibility to learn what that commitment entails. For project-based community-engaged learning, your supervisor or instructor should provide you with a project description that includes expectations, deadlines, points of contact, specs for the final deliverable, and so on. In some cases, part of your project might be to create the project description based on preliminary conversations with your community partner. If you're responsible for articulating the project scope, expectations, deadlines, and deliverables, you should compose a draft overview of these items immediately after your meeting with your site supervisor and share it with him or her to ensure accuracy.

Now, before we move on, let's just talk about the elephant in the room—your phone. We all love the comfort of pulling out our phones to check our social media accounts, e-mail, and sports scores. We get so much joy from how we use our phones. And yet we can also acknowledge collectively that our phones create barriers between us. They divert our attention from the people who are physically present in the spaces we occupy. They provide an escape from necessarily dealing with moments of discomfort and difficult interactions. They offer a quick (or not so quick) diversion from arduous tasks. In other words, they are particularly problematic in the context of community-engaged learning, where we are supposed to be interacting with other people, seeking out new learning, and contributing to the work of our host organizations. Thus, we implore you to exercise great discretion in how and when you use your phone while in community. We aren't telling you to turn it off and put it away, although perhaps, as we suggested earlier, your host organization may have regulations that require such action. We are just telling you to be mindful of when, how, and why you are using your phone during your community engagement and adjust your phone use to reflect dispositions of commitment, empathy, and intellectual curiosity. For example, if you need your phone because your children's school might call to tell you they are sick, or your grandparent is in the hospital and you are waiting for a status update, let your supervisor know that you might receive a call and that you will need to excuse yourself to take it in a location where it won't bother others.

Communication

Communication is so important in community-engaged learning that it warrants its own distinct set of responsibilities. Note that this section is specifically about professional communication with your instructor and the staff overseeing you at your host organization.

Explicit communication of expectations, limitations, strengths, and concerns is an extremely helpful place to start a new relationship. This applies to not only the community-engaged course but also other aspects of our lives as well. Imagine how much more smoothly our relationships with family and romantic partners would go if we created space to talk about these things before conflict arose. Imagine how much more successful you could be in class if you and your instructor had perfect clarity about the alignment or tension between your expectations and theirs.

Shifting our focus back to your community-engaged course, you'll find that your instructor and site supervisor will do their best to communicate all the relevant details when the course begins. It is likely that your instructor's expectations are communicated in the syllabus and perhaps in one of the first lectures. Similarly, it's common for community partners to express their understanding of the community-engaged learning arrangement in the form of a student learning contract or memorandum of understanding that you may have to read and sign. Whereas syllabi and contracts may seem like iron-clad mandates, community-engaged learning requires flexibility and responsiveness in order to account for multiple constituents' expectations and needs. If you have questions or concerns from the beginning, share them with your instructor and/or site supervisor so they can provide additional information.

Unfortunately, even when we attempt to set a strong foundation through open communication from the beginning, challenges will still arise. We encourage you to not only recognize this inevitability but also frame it as an opportunity to learn something new. Your responsibility will be to assess the situation and communicate proactively about challenges before they become worse. Just take care not to frame your concerns or frustrations as an attack or admonishment. Rather, communicate them professionally and sincerely in a way that indicates you are seeking support in finding solutions. One framework for thinking and talking about challenging situations is the ORID model (Stanfield, 2000). ORID provides a series of questions to help you organize your thinking in terms of objective (O), reflective (R), interpretive (I), and decisional (D) dimensions.

When thinking objectively about a situation, the purpose is to describe exactly what happened. What was the progression of events? Who said what? What is the current reality of the situation? What did you observe? Moving to the reflective component means identifying the feelings and emotions connected with the experience. How does this situation make you feel and how might others be feeling about it? In what ways are this situation and the associated feelings similar to others you've experienced? Combining the objective information and reflective considerations can lead you to interpret the situation more clearly. What is each constituent's ultimate goal? What is the underlying cause of the challenge? What factors, opportunities, and limitations do we need to consider when addressing the issue? This systematic analysis can lead to questions that shape decisions about how to move forward. What options do we have for addressing the challenge? What is a mutually acceptable outcome? Who needs to be involved in devising and carrying out a solution? What are potential limitations and constraints to our efforts? How will we know if we've achieved a positive outcome? How will this situation cause me to act differently in the future? These are all just examples of an endless array of questions you might ask and answer within the ORID framework as you navigate challenging situations in your community-engaged course. You can use these questions for your own personal reflection (more on that in a bit) but also as prompts for conversations with your instructor, peers, and community partner. Note that this framework can be especially helpful when a situation seems heated or tense because it guides you through a process of intentional communication rather than allowing the discussion to be driven by the natural human tendency to cast blame and act defensively when issues arise.

As a final note on the importance of communication, we want to distinguish and honor the practice of receiving feedback throughout the community-engaged experience and as it culminates. It is a beneficial professional practice to gather information from others about how they perceive your performance. It demonstrates a commitment to learning and growth. It conveys humility and a desire to succeed. In many cases, feedback can be really gratifying because it reinforces our belief that we've added value to a situation through our contributions. But it also means that you might hear things about yourself that don't feel so great, which is why so many of us avoid or dismiss opportunities to collect feedback.

Whether you solicit it or not, you will likely receive feedback from a number of constituents in the community-engaged experience. Of course, in the most traditional sense of feedback in the context of academia, you'll receive grades from your instructor, indicating your level of achievement on class assignments. Many instructors also ask community partners to do a performance evaluation for students and use the responses to help them determine final grades. However, we believe that a mere grade can be a somewhat unhelpful form of feedback both because it doesn't tell you what you did right or wrong and it does not tell you how to improve. What would be more valuable? Specific feedback on what you did well, what you could improve, and how you might adjust your performance to be more effective in the future.

We know it can be scary to make yourself vulnerable to critique. We don't know anyone who genuinely enjoys hearing about things they don't do so well. But remember how we talked in the previous chapter about the importance of embracing moments of discomfort? Remember how these moments can signal that our worldview might not align with how the world really works? That applies to the way we see ourselves too. Receiving critical feedback can be uncomfortable, unless we recognize that it's a necessary part of the professional development process, especially when we're engaging in tasks that require us to develop new competencies. It's possible that your site supervisor will invite you to engage in activities that are new and different, meaning you may struggle to perform effectively at the beginning, warranting corrective feedback.

Consider an activity like canvassing, going door to door to collect signatures for a petition. It seems like it could be easy—walk around the neighborhood, knock on doors, ask people to sign the paper on your clipboard. Of course, if you've done canvassing before, you know there's so much more to it. You have to follow a strategic map so that you don't knock on the same doors as the other canvasser who was assigned to the next block. You have to learn how to give a quick elevator pitch for the issue you are petitioning about because people will grow impatient if you launch into a long-winded and fumbling description. You have to anticipate and be prepared for follow-up questions from residents. You need to keep track of which homes you've visited and how many signatures you've collected. You have to problem-solve challenges that arise like language barriers or guard dogs. These actions probably don't come easy to many of us. We have to learn how to do them as we move through the experience. We may make mistakes, and it's a gift when someone points them out and advises us about how to correct them. Thus, we encourage you to seek feedback from others throughout your community-engaged course. Ask your peers how they perceive your level of engagement with community. Invite your site supervisor to observe your work and offer insights and advice. If you receive positive feedback, you'll be affirmed to know that you're adding value through your efforts. If you receive critical feedback, fight the urge to get defensive and justify the behavior. Instead, allow the discomfort to be a signal that there's something new to learn from this situation. And then move into reflection mode.

Critical Reflection

Let's start with what critical reflection *isn't*. It's a common misconception that reflection in community-engaged learning means expressing one's feelings about doing service and/or learning about the community. To be sure, our feelings play an important role in how we make sense of the world, but naming those feelings is only one step toward explaining our learning. We need to develop a practice of *critical reflection*, which "requires questioning assumptions and values, and paying attention to the impacts and implication of our community work" (Mitchell, 2008). The fodder for this type of reflection is the spectrum of information you've gained from classroom and academic sources like lectures and texts, community sources like direct observation of service delivery and conversations with community members, and your previous life experiences. You must take in, analyze, and synthesize this information to generate new understandings about yourself, your community, social justice issues, and academic course content. Reflection is not only an important practice for community-engaged learning but also a valuable life skill.

Although most of us have never been explicitly taught how to practice critical reflection, community-engaged courses should be structured to support you in developing this skill. In fact, reflection is meant to happen multiple times and in various ways throughout the term. You will reflect before, during, and after your community engagement experiences. You will reflect alone and with others. You will reflect in formal and informal ways. You might be invited to reflect through journaling, structured written assignments, group discussions, interactive activities, simulations, or case studies. These reflection assignments will probably require you to respond to questions that go beyond asking what you did in the community and how you felt about it.

Ideally, the questions will prompt you to think about the complexity of community dynamics and justice issues, and you will not be able to come up with easy answers. Rather, your answers will need to reflect an inclusive and nuanced understanding that is justified with facts, scholarship, and direct experience. You will need to examine the root causes and intersections of issues, the forces that shape communities, and the impact of systemic and individual social change interventions. We are guessing your community-engaged experience will leave you with more questions than answers, which is a good thing. Use your intellectual curiosity to continue to ask and seek answers to questions even as you move on from your community-engaged course.

In addition to critically thinking about community and justice, you'll engage in reflection about how your community experience challenges, reinforces, exemplifies, and/or defies the disciplinary concepts and theories you learned in class. You may be asked to analyze the work of your host organization using a particular theoretical framework or describe the merits and limitations of philosophical arguments about social constructs. More concretely, nursing students might reflect on how symptoms of a particular health issue present in diverse patients, preservice teachers might reflect on the effectiveness of classroom management strategies in after-school programs, or computer science students could compare and contrast technical factors that contribute to the digital divide in urban and rural communities.

Finally, you'll have the opportunity to reflect on your own identity, values, beliefs, and commitments in light of your new learning experiences. This practice builds on what we explained in the previous chapter about how people's dispositions and worldviews evolve and shift. Critical reflection will guide you to examine the extent to which new experiences and information align with what you believe to be true. The experiences and information that are familiar to you will probably be comfortably integrated into your mind as reinforcements of what you believe. The new and unfamiliar experiences will likely generate feelings of discomfort, signaling to you that there's a disconnect between what you believe and what you've experienced. Reflection will help you determine whether the new experiences and information warrant a change in the way you think about the world.

The next chapter profiles four students who describe the ways community-engaged learning helped them develop new and valuable knowledge, skills, and dispositions. Essentially, these students are modeling reflection by explicitly articulating the learning they gained from their experience.

5

TRANSFORMATIONS

How Community-Engaged Learning
Changes Us

Type "transformation" and "community-engaged learning" into Google and you will get 12,400 results in less than a second. Type "transformation" and "service-learning," a particular kind of community-engaged learning, and watch as Google retrieves a whopping 600,000 results. Clearly there is a connection between community-engaged learning and transformation. The title of this book refers to transformative learning. Maybe that led you to believe something would happen marking a milestone in life, a point at which you would always be able to look and say your life was one thing before and a very different thing afterward. That might happen, but it's also a very tall order for community-engaged learning. Most of us have only a few such moments in our lives. If colleges and universities could make such life-changing moments a guaranteed, regular feature of community-engaged courses, they would be doing it and advertising it as one of the main benefits of higher education.

As you can tell, this kind of momentous change is not what you should expect. Then why do books like this and professors and students engaged in community-engaged learning call it transformational? What do they mean when they talk about transformative learning? What makes transformative learning happen? And who and what is transformed by community-engaged learning? This final chapter will explore some of those questions and introduce you to four students reflecting on how their community-engaged experiences were transformative. Although they may not use that language in their stories, after reading this chapter, you should be able to identify some of the ways their learning was transformative and, in the process, make yourself open to similar kinds of experiences.

What Is Transformative Learning?

First of all, what does *transformation* mean and what is *transformative learning*? If you look for a definition of *transformation*, the emphasis is on dramatic change of a large scale. Think of the metamorphosis from a caterpillar to a butterfly. That's a transformation. It results in something entirely new, something irreversible that cannot be undone. The change is permanent and life altering.

Is transformation always such a big thing? In common parlance, it often is. But when we describe transformative learning, perhaps we set ourselves up for disappointment if we expect change on such a huge, life-changing scale. It makes sense instead to think of transformative learning not so much in terms of how big the change is as it does to think in terms of what changes and how. Jack Mezirow (1997) is a scholar who has spent a career researching and theorizing transformative learning. He defines *transformative learning* as "a process of effecting change in a *frame of reference*" (p. 5). Frames of reference might include habits of mind, which are "broad abstract, orienting, habitual ways of thinking, feeling, and acting influenced by assumptions that constitute a set of codes" (pp. 5–6). He describes how habits of mind "become articulated in a specific point of view—the constellation of belief, value judgment, attitude, and feeling that shapes a particular interpretation" (p. 6). Transformative learning, or a change in our frame of reference, is a result of critical reflection on the assumptions that inform our habits of mind and points of view. For example, if you have ever had a learning experience that helped you see how power and privilege operate in society and changed how you looked at everything from that point on, then you've had a transformative learning experience. Maybe you used to think some kinds of jokes that mocked certain people were funny, but then you had an experience that helped you empathize and think differently. Suddenly those jokes were never funny again. That's a change in frame of reference and an example of transformative learning.

For Mezirow, *transformative learning* is defined by what changes—our way of thinking, knowing, understanding, and making sense of the world—and how it changes through reflection on our own thinking and understanding. Contrast this to transformation that is defined mostly in terms of outward manifestations of change—choosing a major in college, deciding on a particular career track, changing how one looks or presents oneself in the world. These outward manifestations of change may be the product of transformative learning, but—big as those changes might seem to those looking at them—they may also be the product of following a trend or copying an admired authority figure, processes that lack the change in frame of reference that Mezirow describes as fundamental.

Community-engaged learning provides opportunities for reflection that can lead to a change in a frame of reference. Watch the video clip in Figure 5.1 (3 minutes), "Seeing the World Through a New Lens," in which Kristian describes his community-engaged learning experience during a summer in India. Look for evidence of transformative learning.

Figure 5.1.   Seeing the world through a new lens.

Note: See video at https://vimeo.com/236989805/a28a703fea

Kristian's learning wasn't "big" in the sense of life altering, but it was powerful because he started to see things differently, and in that sense, it is a transformation. He describes changes in what he thinks he is capable of doing—tolerating heat, eating as a vegetarian. But probably more important, Kristian describes how his thinking changed. He challenged his assumptions of what it means to be a woman in a poor and traditional society. Whereas before he might only have seen a woman as "oppressed" because she always had to do the cooking, he could now see someone who had autonomy and agency as evidenced by the way she cooked and because of what preparing a meal meant to her. Kristian challenged what was "engrained" in him or what Mezirow would call his habit of mind about women in developing countries. Through reflection on his lived experience, he developed a new point of view about his host mother. Similarly, he developed a different frame of reference about mental illness while in India. Although mental illness is often seen as dangerous or something to be scared of in the United States, he noticed that it was viewed differently in India. In this case, Kristian's frame of reference has not shifted, but it might be in the process of shifting. Something has been "sparked" for him and he continues to explore how to understand mental health.

Kristian's story illustrates the importance of reflection. He wasn't changed by experience, but by his thinking about what the experience meant. Reflection was part of how he came to make sense of his community-engaged experience. Rather than come in only with preconceived ideas about what he was meant to do in community, he describes how he talked with members of the community or went fishing with them to understand what they needed and how he could be most useful. He advises people following him to "feel before they think," "build a community relationship first," and learn by listening. That process allowed him to understand a culture different from his own and be transformed in the process.

What Does the Arc of Transformation Look Like?

Kristian's story is inspiring, but it is also unusual. Most of you reading this book will not spend a summer in India as part of your community-engaged learning. More typically, you will work locally for a semester or quarter on issues that are of importance across the United States, issues like educational inequity or environmental degradation. Homelessness is another such issue, one that Dylan addressed during her college years. Working in the community on issues of homelessness, Dylan used her community-engaged learning experiences to challenge stereotypes. As you watch the video clip in Figure 5.2 (2 minutes) where she describes her experiences, notice the timeline for the kinds of transformations that Dylan describes in herself and in the community where she worked.

Figure 5.2. Challenging stereotypes.

Note: See video at https://vimeo.com/236989748/bfeaa66624

Dylan talks about the rhetoric around homelessness that she grew up with. She also describes how she challenged that frame of reference and shifted to a place where she drew on a different set of assumptions about people who are homeless, where she learned, as she says, "There's always more to the story." Dylan's transformative learning experience was not a single "aha" moment. She reflects as a senior on where she was as a first-year student and where she ended up in her thinking four years later. That tells us something about the arc of transformative learning. Although there may be a moment or spark that gets transformation in motion, it often unfolds over time through continued engagement and reflection. From a self-described deficit notion of seeing people who are homeless as lazy or on drugs, Dylan came to see all the variability in how people become homeless. She uses words like *love*, *art*, *strength*, and *resilience* to describe a community of persons who are homeless, terms that are not usually associated in the popular frame of reference with homelessness. She credits her changed frame of reference with allowing her to be an activist and an ally.

Notice not only how Dylan changed her frame of reference about people who are homeless but also how change is made. Like many people who see injustice and are eager to work for change, Dylan started her community-engaged learning with the idea that she could change the world in a semester. Without letting herself off the hook, she sees that change takes a longer commitment. Her focus for thinking about what changes as a result of community-engaged learning shifted from external changes she would make in the lives of others to thinking about internal changes that would shape her thinking about who she is in the world and, ultimately, how effective she might be as an agent of change. These changes are not the kind that happen in most learning experiences. Think of a class lecture you attended, for example. Chances are you learned things you did not previously know about the topic. You added to your body of knowledge. All those lectures over the course of a semester can make a considerable contribution to what you know, but they may not change in any fundamental way how you view the world. Community-engaged learning has greater potential for transformative learning because it is immersive and speaks to feelings and intellect. Dylan's story illustrates how that potential can take time. We hope that the questions your community-engaged learning experience raises stick with you and inspire you to action for more than a semester or quarter.

What Supports Transformation?

In her first year of college, Dylan began a commitment to community engagement that extended throughout her four years. For any number of reasons, you may not be able to continue your community engagement in any formal way. The transformation may be less in the community than in your own habits of mind and point of view. Dylan suggests this when she talks about her realization that she wasn't going to change the world in a semester.

Although you may not continue working with a particular community organization, you can allow yourself to continue thinking about questions that are raised by your community-engaged learning experience. Reflection is characteristic of community-engaged learning, and your instructor should provide you with formal opportunities to reflect individually and collectively on your experiences. After a community-engaged course ends, however, you still have opportunities to reflect in less formal ways. We hope your community-engaged learning experience provides questions that stick with you and frames of reference that continue to help you make meaning of the world and act with integrity and intention. Watch the video clip in Figure 5.3 (2 minutes) where Lionell describes how his community-engaged learning experience was transformative.

Figure 5.3. Building relationships.

Note: See video at https://vimeo.com/236989725/2511838613

Lionell rethought who might be a "problem child." He described having an open mind-set. That openness informed his lasting take-away from community-engaged learning—the importance of building relationships to accomplish important goals. In this case, the goal was to support a child's academic learning. Lionell realized that change takes place in the context of relationships and that, without them, he could not accomplish any other end. Because he built a relationship, he was able to see how the child with whom he was working learned. He viewed the relationship as reciprocal. He had things to learn as much as he had things to teach.

Lionell's story illustrates the habits of mind that serve reflection: open-mindedness, respect, flexibility, and reciprocity. His story also illustrates the importance of relationships. None of us can do our community-engaged work in isolation. Our learning comes from the interactions we have with others and the relationships we develop.

Who or What Is Transformed?

Relationships matter to community-engaged learning, and the best relationships are those that are reciprocal. Perhaps you have been in relationships that did not feel reciprocal—a relationship where someone else did all the talking and you only got to listen, for example. A reciprocal relationship would be one where both persons talk and listen, where both have a voice and are heard. In terms of service-learning, reciprocal means not just that each party gets something or gives something—like the student giving service and gaining wisdom, and the community partner getting help and sharing knowledge—but that the relationship is one that meets each where their strengths and needs are. As mentioned in chapter 2, we can sometimes get caught up in roles during community-engaged learning, especially if it is framed as service-learning. That frame may set us up for feeling like we need to be contributing something exceptional. Sometimes our own enthusiasm for transforming the community can shape our beliefs about the actions we need to take in community-engaged learning. Watch Mary's story in Figure 5.4 (2 minutes) to see how her community-engaged learning experience helped her reframe what it meant to change the world through community-engaged learning.

Figure 5.4. Finding your place.

Note: See video at https://vimeo.com/236989773/0293cd46f9

When Mary started working with her community partner, she had certain ideas about what she should do to make a difference. Her goal was to change the world—which is, in fact, part of the tagline for the university where she studies. She was disappointed to be making phone calls for her organization. Some of us might feel the same way, either because we believe we have more to contribute or we believe more needs to be done. Mary was able to change her point of view to see this work from the perspective of her community partner. As a result, she came to understand why it was important to the organization, to see how a seemingly small and simple act could have an important and valued outcome for the organization.

When you think of community-engaged learning as transformative, your first thoughts may have gone to what that transformation looks like for the community, how you would make a difference in an organization or in the community or in tackling a social problem.

Again, remember that we tend to think of transformation as being on a big scale. Mary, like Dylan in the earlier video clip, reminds us to be humble about the difference we make in the community. We should not think of those contributions as insignificant or unimportant, especially if what we are doing is meeting needs as identified and expressed by the community. We may do well, however, to enter community-engaged learning without the mind-set of transforming others or transforming the world, especially if the community we are entering is different from our own. When we do that, we run the risk of taking on a savior mentality, of negatively exercising privilege that can stand in the way of our learning and meeting community-identified needs.

The delicate balance in community-engaged learning is to enter with an open mind for your own learning, with humility to understand you may not change the world, and yet with the resolve not to prioritize your own learning so much that the difference you make in the community is negligible. As scholars like Randy Stoecker (2016) have pointed out, too often community voices have been ignored in service-learning or community-engaged learning. Too often the success of community-engaged learning is measured only in terms of what students get out of it, not the community (Stoecker, 2016; Stoecker & Tryon, 2009).

You may feel like you're being asked to live with a paradox—remember that your contribution is small and that community engagement should somehow make a difference beyond your own learning. Notice how Mary does that by recognizing that what the community is asking her to do may not be what she wants to do, that the bigger picture of what the community wants may be different from her more immediate desire to get involved in certain preconceived ways. It helped that Mary saw connections to struggles in her own community. When we see the struggle of those in the community connected to our own liberation or our own well-being, the balance between what we hope to get out of community-engaged learning and what we hope to contribute is easier to maintain. This is related to another delicate balance—maintaining humility about not changing the world with a sense of urgency in the face of social injustice. As you can see in the stories of students describing their learning, they maintain personal humility without giving up a commitment to making a difference. As you think about your own community-engaged learning, think about how you can maintain your humility and commitment to making a difference on issues that may feel very urgent to you right now.

How to Prepare for Transformational Learning

As the stories of students in this chapter illustrate, transformational learning can change your worldview across a number of different domains, including political views, moral stances, intellectual framing, cultural lenses, and personal and spiritual beliefs. Kristian shifted his personal frame of reference for his own capacity to live in another culture and question his cultural norms as he reflected on the mother in his host family. Dylan changed her intellectual understanding of homelessness and her political and moral beliefs about how to show up as an ally and advocate. Lionell came to a new intellectual and personal understanding about how to reframe what it means for a child to be a "problem." Mary saw her worldview about change-making shift as she worked with those in her own community.

Across different kinds of transformations, these students exhibited some common characteristics that can serve as models as you engage in your own community-engaged learning. You read about these characteristics, or dispositions, in chapter 3. These characteristics manifest as listening and observing, keeping an open mind, paying attention to relationships, and integrating questions and habits of mind from community-engaged learning into the narrative of your life. Think about how you already exhibit these characteristics and think about where circumstances can make them challenging— for example, at the end of the semester when the crush of paper deadlines makes it hard to spend time listening to others.

All the cases here represent students who listened and looked carefully. Kristian really looked at how his host mother saw her place in the world. He listened, sometimes in the most informal settings, to how members of the community defined their strengths and needs. Dylan looked to see beauty and art in a neighborhood where others might see only poverty and other social problems. She listened to the stories of people who are homeless. Lionell observed the student he was supposed to tutor to figure out how best to support him as a learner. He listened to him with the mind-set that he had something to learn. Mary looked at the organization where she was working to see what they needed rather than for opportunities to do what she wanted. She listened to ideas in the community and the classroom and brought them together to make sense of her experience.

Related to listening and observing carefully is keeping an open mind. All the students introduced to you in this chapter explicitly mentioned the importance of this characteristic or demonstrated it through their actions. Kristian kept an open mind so he could understand and challenge his notions of oppression and agency for women. Dylan kept an open mind about persons who are homeless so she could question the rhetoric about poverty and homelessness around which she had grown up. Lionell kept an open mind about what the student with whom he was assigned to work could accomplish and learn. Mary kept an open mind about her place in the community and as an agent of change.

In all these cases, keeping an open mind served transformative learning. Keeping an open mind is something we want to believe is possible. These stories illustrate it is possible, but they may not fully present the difficulty of doing so. We all grow up with deeply embedded ideas. We hold on to values that become entrenched. Sometimes we cannot even see that we've closed off other possible ways to see the world because of our blinders. When you catch yourself operating with blinders, remember not to be hard on yourself but to appreciate the values of what you gained from reflection. The best way to keep an open mind is through questions. A great prompt for reflection is to ask, "How do I know this?" and to apply this question even to the ideas and understandings that seem self-evident. As you start to peel away at how you know, you may see new opportunities for understanding differently.

Building relationships is another common marker across all these stories of students' transformative learning. Their transformed understanding happened in the context of relationships

—relationships with community members including those they were serving, community organizations, and persons on campus as well. Building relationships means prioritizing time for getting to know others, treating people with respect, hearing their points of view, and meeting them where they are. Notice how building a relationship meant Lionell took his responsibilities further than was required by his instructor. He went from tutoring one student to leading a whole group of students on a tour of campus. And because he was focusing on the relationship with the student he was tutoring rather than their roles, he was able to blur the lines of those serving and being served, those learning and those teaching. If you are providing indirect service from an office, like Mary, there are opportunities to build relationships with everyone on staff, not just your supervisor. You can develop networks with people who are knowledgeable and passionate about an issue.

Relationships can also be with an entire community as well as individuals. Kristian advises those in a community-engaged learning program to "build a community relationship first." A relationship with community can be the sum of many relationships with individuals in a community. It also benefits, however, from knowledge about a community's history and social/economic context. None of us are isolated individuals, and understanding the larger context of where people live is part of building relationships with community. As you begin your community-engaged learning, look for the opportunities to build relationships rather than just getting some service done, to know individuals and a community rather than only writing a paper about people generally and a place abstractly.

All these students left with questions or new understandings. They managed to integrate what they were reflecting on into the narratives of their lives. Kristian used his experience in India to understand mental health more deeply, to change ideas about agency and autonomy for people who are poor. Dylan's community-engaged learning sparked ideas about activism and allyship. Lionell talked about how his understanding that people learn in different ways has stuck with him. Mary's community-engaged learning enabled her to see connections between community and classroom—among struggles of communities, her own sense of self, and her place as an actor in history. These understandings are retrospective and tell us something about how transformation happens. Although it might come in a flash during a moment in the community or the classroom, it is more likely to come to us after the fact as we look back on what we have done, whom we have met and come to know, and what questions we find ourselves continuing to ask. We encourage you to think of your community-engaged learning experience as less of a discrete experience from which you will gain something and then move on and more of an opportunity to do something meaningful that weaves into the larger web of your life.

Kristian, Dylan, Lionell, and Mary present a picture of transformational learning that acknowledges the knowledge and wisdom that any learner brings to community-engaged learning. Although some people think of transformational learning as a big "aha" moment of change in one direction from complete lack of understanding to an incredible new depth, these students illustrate something different. They show that transformational learning does not assume learners start out with no ideas or the "wrong" ideas. Rather they come to a community-engaged learning experience with their lived experience and the insight that comes from making sense of it. Community-engaged learning allows students to further question that experience and challenge some assumptions by broadening experience, deepening understanding of the context of community, and introducing theoretical perspectives to understand issues affecting society— community members as well as you and your classmates. Just as good community-engaged learning focuses on the assets of a community rather than its deficits, it also builds on the assets of students rather than supposing they come only with deficits or "blank slates" on which new knowledge is inscribed.

The students presented in this chapter illustrate that transformational learning is also complex. Challenging simplistic notions that transformation from community-engaged learning experiences means moving in one simple direction from what Kahne and Westheimer (1999) call a charity orientation to a change orientation, Strain (2006) likens this deficit thinking about students to the deficit thinking about communities that we hope to avoid. He compares transformational learning to the movement of a starfish and offers it as a metaphor to better explain what transformation might look like. For a starfish, "there is no forward or back, left or right, no 'either/or.' Instead movement can be in multiple and shifting directions" (p. 1). Using this metaphor, you can see that learning does not fall into dichotomous categories, with certain categories like forward or change usually privileged over others like backward or charity. Instead, learning from community engagement might allow you to explore more deeply the worldview you already have. Over time, that exploration may lead down the road to different frames of reference. It may also confirm a frame of reference. Confirmation can be transformational if it means being able to draw on other ways of knowing or new information to understand habits of mind or points of view.

Finally, we hope community-engaged learning transforms not only your way of thinking but also your actions, whether personal, professional, or civic. In the personal realm, we hope your community-engaged learning leaves you with a set of questions to which you return throughout your life. We hope it leaves you with a disposition to think about what's good for society, not just good for you. You may find yourself asking such questions years later when you are deciding where to live or where to send your child to school. You may find yourself volunteering for organizations that are a continuation of community engagement from your college years.

Professionally, you may find your career trajectory shaped by your community-engaged experience. One obvious way is by choosing to work in the nonprofit or public sector. If you work for a large corporation, you may find your community-engaged experience shapes how you make decisions and how you treat others.

We know that some students see engagement with community as an alternative to political engagement (Colby, Beaumont, Ehrlich, & Corngold, 2007). We also know that student activism is increasing as students realize the need to be leaders of change on campus and in community. We hope that part of your transformation is taking learning from community engagement about social issues and political questions and using that learning as you engage in political processes from voting to setting political agendas and advocating for policies that you believe will make the world more just and equitable.

AFTERWORD

When I was meandering through life after high school, I did not think I had many experiences in my youth that I would have considered significant transformational moments. I most certainly was not equipped to believe that my perceived lack of experiences would eventually lead to a vocation in the field of community engagement. In fact, when I was growing up in North Hollywood, I accepted being invisible and felt most comfortable not being seen, partly because a core Filipino value is the concept of others before self, and as a first-generation immigrant my goal was to blend in and not be seen. It was also because I did not have the ability to see the assets in myself and in my community. I accepted this because I knew no other way. Although I now realize that I had a vibrant community teaching me values about myself and others, I did not fully embrace my "beloved community," a concept that Dr. Martin Luther King Jr. originated to describe his vision of peaceful coexistence and equitable interdependence among a diverse population and bell hooks (2003) extended as an aspirational model for modern social change. As a young person I did not understand the tools of reflection, asset thinking, and dispositional discernment as outlined by the authors in this book. If I could go back in time and employ the tools articulated in the *Student Companion to Community-Engaged Learning* such as being a reflective practitioner I would have realized much sooner that my "beloved community" was all around me, a community comprising family, friendships, and a vibrant group of people of all colors and identities.

Fast forward to many years later. I realized that I had to embrace what Pulitzer Prize–winning journalist Jose Vargas urged when he said you have to "run toward yourself" (2011). As a journalist he often reported on injustices in the world while compartmentalizing the inner turmoil he was facing. Vargas's inner conflict was rooted in the fact that he learned he was undocumented in high school while trying to obtain a driver's license. He eventually disclosed his immigration status in a 2011 article in the *New York Times Sunday Magazine,* and it was at that moment that Vargas decided to "run toward himself," a process he said was much more difficult than coming out as a gay man. *The Student Companion to Community-Engaged Learning* reminds us that our experiences, no matter how big or small, deeply impact how we make meaning in our lives. When created with intention and purpose, community-engaged experiences not only link theory with practice but also powerfully exemplify the promise of higher education that gives all of us a chance to run toward ourselves.

For students reading this book, heed the authors' question about what you hope to gain from your community-engaged experiences. By asking this thoughtful question at the very beginning of your community-engaged experiences, you can enter into what Ellen Langer describes as "mindful attending" (Ruark, 2010). Langer (2014) suggests that this act of mindfulness informs context and perspective and is the "essence of engagement." The authors remind us that thoughtful questioning and engaging in critical reflection are necessary for creating a lifelong practice of becoming a reflective professional and participant in civic life. The authors face head on the most urgent issues that affect communities and encourage us to embrace the notion that it is through reciprocal relationships that one earns the privilege of working alongside leaders in the community, not as saviors but as partners. As you begin your journey in the community, this book will serve as a meditative companion and roadmap on how to move past feelings of being overwhelmed by the injustices in the world. When used as a guide, this book will help you develop a daily practice of discovering assets in yourself and your community, and it will lead you to a destination that experiences community engagement as "desire-centered" work.

This book is also an important guide for faculty. As leaders in the field of equity and inclusion, civic education, and community-engaged scholarship, the authors bring extensive knowledge and expertise that will serve all faculty. The authors hold an inclusive definition of *all faculty* that includes full- or part-time faculty, professors of practice, and wisdom holders in the community who serve as culture bearers and create the conditions to bridge the space between town and gown. That space created in between is what Daloz Parks, Parks Daloz, and Keen (1997) describe as "the commons." The commons is where community-engaged pedagogy and practice fit best because the commons acknowledges that the process of inquiry, knowledge creation, and the understanding of where wisdom resides are cocreated with the community. This necessarily means faculty must take up the challenge of creating transformative experiences for students and contributing to positive community change in collaboration with community coeducators. The authors are right that "landmines" exist, and this is especially true for faculty who consider community engagement as "extra" or "add-on" rather than an integration of engaged scholarship. However, this book weaves together decades of best practices from the field of community engagement, reminding us that faculty who thrive in this space are those who create the conditions for students and community to join in the "commons."

The authors encourage us to integrate the lessons in this book into a daily practice that builds on self-discovery, community relationships, and transformational change. When I reflect on my own self-discovery of "running toward myself," I have come to welcome the sacred practice of discernment as a core process of practicing the principles of community engagement beyond the classroom. The authors reinforce how self-discovery shifts our gaze from a deficit- to asset-based lens in order to "fully embrace who you are." Woven into the book are important narratives from diverse community voices that passionately express how the "self" fully examined is the foundation for the kind of mutuality that creates strong and reciprocal community partnerships. A friend once told me you can't do the "we" work unless you do the "I" work first; it is through the process of discernment that conditions are created to manifest a collective vision between self and community. Lastly, the authors address the "why" of building a strong practice and culture of community engagement in higher education. In order to truly be change-makers committed to transformation and systems change, community-engaged workers must be part of the core mission of academia. As the report *A Crucible Moment: College Learning & Democracy's Future* (National Task Force on Civic Learning and Democratic Engagement, 2012) implores, academic institutions must

> offer an intellectual and public commons where it is possible not only to theorize about what education for democratic citizenship might require in a diverse society, but also to rehearse that citizenship daily in the fertile, roiling context of pedagogical inquiry and hands-on experience. (p. 2)

The authors recognize and illuminate the many paths to achieve transformation by shining a spotlight on the power of reciprocity and equity that occur with experiences in the community. This book focuses all of us on going beyond the theory, living the practice, and recognizing that community engagement, as Father Greg Boyle (2010) suggests, widens the "circle of compassion" to "imagine no one standing outside that circle" (p. 190). As the circle that we cocreate widens, so does our beloved community.

Chris Nayve
Associate Vice President for Community Engagement,
University of San Diego

A LETTER TO OUR FACULTY COLLEAGUES

Dear colleagues,

Thank you for your commitment to learning that goes beyond the walls of a classroom, and thank you for teaching in ways that can serve the ends of social justice by meeting community-identified needs. We take inspiration from colleagues at the University of San Francisco and at other schools and colleges where we have worked. We would not be able to imagine this book without the example of faculty who teach for community-engaged learning every semester.

For those of you who may feel like you are the first at your campus or have not had role models, we offer encouragement and reassurance. You can do this. If the imperatives or responsibilities described in this book seem large, know that they are, but nothing is beyond the ability of faculty who are intentional, flexible, reflective, collaborative, and committed to students. These qualities describe lots of the best teachers, not just faculty committed to community-engaged learning. We suspect you share these dispositions and have much to draw on as you think about teaching with the ideas included in this book. Let us say a little bit more about each disposition.

When we talk about intentional, we mean making community-engaged learning integral to the course you teach, not an add-on that students complete on their own without time in class to frame, unpack, or make meaning from their experience. Most instructors approach their courses with a high degree of intention that is made explicit to students. If nothing else, syllabi require us to think about things like learning outcomes, readings, and assignments. That same degree of intentionality and explicitness is required for community-engaged learning. Although it is harder to control or predict every twist of a community-engaged learning experience, that uncertainty does not lessen the need for forethought, particularly in framing the experience up front. Explicit framing matters because it shapes students' expectations. If students are not told why and how they will engage in community, they may create their own narrative. For example, if you do not explicitly tell students to see the gifts and strengths of a community, they may look for deficits and problems. If you do not emphasize the importance of relationships and processes, students may focus on outcomes like the final project and miss out on developing connections with members of the community, or worse, take advantage of community members for the sake of an assignment.

You should be intentional and explicit in your expectations as well as honest with students about some of the difficulties of community-engaged learning. Students should expect the unexpected and be prepared to solve problems that cannot be imagined at the start of the project. They should know that this is part of the experience and a place for real learning. When you are intentional with students about this expectation, they can see these complications along the way as opportunities to be engaged rather than problems to be dispensed with—by you—as quickly as possible.

As you prepare your students to be flexible, you should be willing and able to practice pragmatism and flexibility as well. Engaged pedagogies require a great deal of power sharing because they are rooted in the assumption that each partner involved with the course has valuable wisdom and a unique story that can contribute to the learning of others. In the classroom, this means making space for students to discuss their engaged experiences, perspectives, critical questions, and new ideas with each other. It means inviting students to speak back to the claims of experts put forth in scholarly journals and other media sources by drawing on their own lived experience and the wisdom that lies in those who live and learn beyond the walls of academia.

Power sharing also means inviting your community partners to work with you as coeducators. There's great value in bringing in your partners' voices during the course design process. They can suggest readings and resources that will help students understand the organizations' work and/or a particular social justice issue. Further, community partners should work with you to codesign the students' community engagement or service experience. Indeed, partners must be invited to articulate their priorities, expectations, needs, and limitations with regard to hosting your students. This ensures that the community-engaged activity is meaningful and beneficial for all parties. Invite community partners into the classroom to provide a student orientation, facilitate reflections, and observe the students' presentations on their engagement activities. Although you won't want to invite community partners to assign grades for the students' engagement activities, you should solicit their feedback on student performance and integrate that into your assessment.

It's also essential to infuse flexibility into how you integrate nondisciplinary content into your course. In other words, in order for students to do community engagement that facilitates learning about social justice issues and builds their capacity for civic engagement, you'll need to provide content that supports such outcomes. This means you might not be able to fit in all the disciplinary content you would otherwise cover in a traditional course. Some of that will need to be swapped out to allow for the readings that frame civic issues, theories of change, and societal systems and structures. As we mentioned before, you'll also need to make time in class for students to discuss their community experiences. Consider replacing some of the time you devote to in-class lectures with time for students to engage in actively synthesizing course content and community-engaged experience.

To successfully implement community-engaged learning, know your students. This is something all good instructors do. When you design a course, even before you have met the students who are still names on a roster, draw on what you know generally about students at your institution and those you have taught in the past. As you think about community-engaged learning, avoid thinking of what Dan Butin (2006) calls the *ideal student*. This student, who is single, White, middle class, between the ages of 18 and 22, able-bodied, going to school full-time, and not working, is not typical of college students. Nonetheless, some faculty members hold this kind of student in mind as they imagine who will be in their course. That's what "ideal" refers to.

One way, then, to know your students is to learn about all the kinds of diversity that exist within a classroom and to develop community-engaged learning experiences that work for students reflecting these diverse backgrounds and experiences. Do not make assumptions, for example, that students know the community they will be engaged in. By the same token, do not assume that all students will be "outsiders." In this text, we have tried to avoid this kind of assumption. Consider that some students will be members of the community, whether it is a geographical community or a community of common affinity, where you are asking students to engage. Remember that students may work 40 hours a week in addition to taking classes. Others may be parents. Many may already be engaged in community through their children's schools, after-school programs, or faith-based institutions. Think about whether your expectations for community engagement, including the hours and the transportation to and from community engagement sites, will work for students who are different from the "ideal."

Think about how students' identities will shape their community-engaged learning experiences. When you think about "safety" in the community or preparing students to encounter "difference" in the community, which students are you thinking about? For some students, safety can mean safe from crime in a neighborhood, whereas for other students, safety can mean safe from police or security who may trail them or make assumptions about why they are there. Some students may encounter many types of difference in community settings compared to environments in which they grew up or previously went to school. Others will feel more at home in community settings and may experience more difference on campus.

Thinking about students also requires taking into account their varied beliefs and experiences. Although college students are caricatured in popular media as more liberal than the population at large, students bring a diversity of social and political opinions into the classroom. Community-engaged learning typically sparks student reflection on social and political issues. Although we take a stand in this text that community-engaged learning should serve social justice goals, we recognize that there are many ways to get there and that students from across a spectrum of beliefs define *justice* differently. Our classrooms need to be places where those differences can be aired and examined.

We invite you to not only learn about your students but also do some self-reflection as well. Donald Schön (1983) introduced the concept of the "reflective practitioner" as a way for professionals to embrace identities as lifelong learners by integrating a reciprocal process of reflection and action to enhance their practice. You can start by considering aspects of your own identity, including how your gender, race, ethnicity, class, ability, and so on have contributed to your beliefs and worldviews. What life experiences were instrumental in your formation as a person, as an educator, and as a member of various communities? To what extent have you engaged with people of diverse identities who have experiences and values that differ from your own? Thinking about your responses to these questions will foster awareness about why and how you think and behave the way you do, including providing insight into why you may have chosen this career path as an educator in a particular discipline.

You can also consider your motivations for teaching a community-engaged course. What is it about this specific way of teaching and learning that seems appropriate to your discipline and intended student outcomes? What are your own civic practices and commitments? How are you engaged in promoting the common good and how might that shape the way you teach your course? What are your strengths and limitations as an educator aspiring to promote student civic engagement? What do you already know and what do you still need to learn about the social justice issues that your students will encounter? Uncovering answers to these questions will have implications for all aspects of your course, and as you'll see, your answers will change with each successive experience.

As you move through the planning and implementation of your community-engaged course, you'll want to continue the cycle of action and reflection. You should note when things go well and when challenges arise, and reflect on the variables that contributed so you can adjust your practice immediately and plan for improvements in future iterations of the course. For example, analyze the extent to which the community-engaged activities helped students achieve the course learning outcomes. Think about which texts and reflection assignments resonated most with the students and which fell flat. Seek feedback from your community partners about their satisfaction with your collaborative efforts and communication style. Engaging in reflection throughout your course can lead to new realizations, practices, and critical questions with regard to your community-engaged teaching.

Although a healthy dose of introspection will contribute to your success, so will your endeavors to reach out to those who can support you. If there are colleagues in your department who teach community-engaged courses, request their syllabi and take them out for coffee to get their advice. If you're the only community-engaged instructor in your department, reach out to peers in other disciplines. Even though you don't share a primary field of expertise, you'll find that you can apply a number of community engagement practices across disciplines. In fact, you may want to draw on the expertise of colleagues as guest speakers in your course to cover aspects of the civic content. We encourage you to seek out your institution's office of community engagement (or the equivalent) to get support and resources from staff. They will likely be able to help you identify community partner organizations, brainstorm appropriate community engagement activities for your course, and develop reflection and assessment assignments. If there's no office of engagement, you can turn to other offices and centers on campus, including your center for teaching excellence and campus cultural centers. You'll likely find no shortage of people who are willing and able to support your efforts.

You can even look beyond your campus to regional, national, and international resources. We suggest connecting with Campus Compact, a consortium of higher education institutions across the United States committed to a public purpose. They produce several publications and also curate a syllabus repository, which you can search by subject. We recommend attending annual conferences like the ones hosted by the International Association for Research on Service-Learning and Community Engagement or Imagining America, which focuses on engaged scholarship in the arts and humanities. If you prefer to do some self-guided professional development, dig into current and past volumes of the *Michigan Journal of Community Service Learning* and the *Journal of Higher Education Outreach and Engagement*. There are also several recent books on community-engaged teaching and scholarship that you can easily find in your campus library or online. In short, there's a vast network of competent and dedicated educators who are teaching innovative community-engaged courses and producing scholarship to inform the practices of their peers.

The fact that you are an educator likely means that you are committed to developing students as persons and scholars who contribute positively to our world. The fact that you want to teach a community-engaged course means that you're probably already predisposed to flexibility, reflexivity, intentionality, and collaboration. Thus, our previous advice is meant to meet you where you're at: embarking on a quest with the best of intentions to teach a course that extends beyond classroom walls and disciplinary boundaries to foster holistic growth and development of your students. You will essentially apply your existing dispositions and competencies to a community-engaged learning framework. Let this book help you lay the foundation for a student learning experience that is rooted in respect, humility, reciprocity, and curiosity. Use it to help your students find their purpose and their place in community as they grapple with the complexities of social justice issues and (re)define their understanding of the common good. Most importantly, recognize that this book is meant to be a companion to you and your students, but it is only one of many companions your students will need on their community-engaged journey. The transformative power of your community-engaged course is bound up in your ability to weave together academic concepts, theories, and studies with community experiences, epistemologies, interactions, and narratives in a way that shapes students' civic worldviews, values, and behaviors.

REFERENCES

Abrams, D. E., & Hogg, M. A. (1990). *Social identity theory: Constructive and critical advances.* New York, NY: Springer-Verlag.

Adams, M. (Ed.). (2000). *Readings for diversity and social justice.* New York, NY: Psychology Press.

Adams, S. (2014, November 12). The 10 skills employers most want in college graduates [Blog]. Retrieved from http://www.forbes.com/sites/susanadams/2014/11/12/the-10-skills-employers-most-want-in-2015-graduates/#19671cf519f6

American Association of Colleges & Universities (AAC&U). (2018). *High-impact practices.* Retrieved from https://www.aacu.org/resources/high-impact-practices

American Civil Liberties Union. (2018). School-to-prison pipeline [Factsheet]. Retrieved from https://www.aclu.org/fact-sheet/locating-school-prison-pipeline?redirect=fact-sheet/what-school-prison-pipeline

American Society of News Editors. (2016, September 9). *2016 survey.* Retrieved from http://asne.org/content.asp?contentid=447

Astin, A. W., Astin, H. S., Lindholm, J. A., Bryant, A. N., Szelényi, K., & Calderone, S. (2005). *The spiritual life of college students: A national study of college students' search for meaning and purpose.* Los Angeles, CA: UCLA Higher Education Research Institute.

Bader, M., & Warkentien, S. (2016). The fragmented evolution of racial integration since the Civil Rights movement. *Sociological Science, 3,* 135–166.

Balingit, M. (2017, December 4). U.S. high school graduation rates rise to new high. *Washington Post.* Retrieved from https://www.washingtonpost.com/news/education/wp/2017/12/04/u-s-high-school-graduation-rates-rise-to-new-high/?utm_term=.9dc126cfa1ad

Barsamian, D. (2004). *Louder than bombs: Interviews from* The Progressive Magazine. Cambridge, MA: South End Press.

Bell, L. A. (2007). Theoretical foundations for social justice education. In M. Adams, L. A. Bell, & P. Griffin (Eds.), *Teaching for diversity and social justice* (2nd ed., pp. 1–14). New York, NY: Routledge.

Bialik, K., & Krogstad, J. M. (2017, January 24). 115th Congress sets new high for racial, ethnic diversity. *Fact Tank.* Retrieved from http://www.pewresearch.org/fact-tank/2017/01/24/115th-congress-sets-new-high-for-racial-ethnic-diversity/

Black Chairmen and CEOs of Fortune 500 Companies. (n.d.). *Black entrepreneurs & executives.* Retrieved from https://www.blackentrepreneurprofile.com/fortune-500-ceos/

Blouin, D. D., & Perry, E. M. (2009). Whom does service learning really serve? Community-based organizations' perspectives on service learning. *Teaching Sociology, 37*(2), 120–135.

Boyle, G. (2010). *Tattoos on the heart: The power of boundless compassion.* New York, NY: Free Press.

Butin, D. (2006). The limits of service-learning in higher education. *The Review of Higher Education, 29*(4), 473–498.

Center for American Women and Politics. (2018). Women in the US Congress 2018 [Factsheet]. Retrieved from http://www.cawp.rutgers.edu/women-us-congress-2017

Colby, A., Beaumont, E., Ehrlich, T., & Corngold, J. (2007). *Educating for democracy: Preparing undergraduates for responsible political engagement.* San Francisco, CA: Jossey-Bass.

Cronley, C., Madden, E., & Davis, J. B. (2015). Making service-learning partnerships work: Listening and responding to community partners. *Journal of Community Practice, 23*(2), 274–289.

Cruz, N. (1994, November 11). *Reexamining service-learning in an international context.* Paper presented at the Annual Conference of the National Society for Experiential Education, Washington DC.

Daloz Parks, S., Parks Daloz, L. A., Keen, J. P. (1997). *Common fire: Leading lives of commitment in a complex world.* Boston, MA: Beacon Press.

Davidson, J. (2016, May 23). High tech firms lag in diversity, EEOC says. *Washington Post.* Retrieved from https://www.washingtonpost.com/news/powerpost/wp/2016/05/23/high-tech-firms-lag-in-diversity-eeoc-says/

Desmond, M. (2016). *Evicted: Poverty and profit in the American city.* New York, NY: Crown.

Dewey, J. (1916). *Democracy and education.* New York, NY: Macmillan.

Dey, E. L., Ott, M. C., Antonaros, M., Barnhardt, C. L., & Holsapple, M. A. (2009). *Engaging diverse viewpoints; What is the campus climate for perspective-taking?* Washington DC: American Association of Colleges and Universities.

Donahue, D. M. (2014). Learning from Harvey Milk: The limits and opportunities of one hero to teach about LGBTQ people and issues. *The Social Studies, 105*(1), 36–44.

Erb, R. (2015, October 11). Young doctor takes on Flint water fight. *USA Today*. Retrieved from http://www.usatoday.com/story/news/nation-now/2015/10/11/flint-water-doctor/73777352/

Eyler, J., Giles, D., & Braxton, J. (1997). The impact of service-learning on college students. *Michigan Journal of Community Service Learning, 4*(1), 5–15.

Free Press. (n.d.). *Diversity in media ownership*. Retrieved from http://www.freepress.net/diversity-media-ownership

Garza, A. (2014, October 7). A herstory of the #Black Lives Matter movement by Alicia Garza. *Feminist Wire*. Retrieved from http://www.thefeministwire.com/2014/10/blacklivesmatter-2/

Gelman, A., Fagan, J., & Kiss, A. (2012). An analysis of the New York City police department's "stop-and-frisk" policy in the context of claims of racial bias. *Journal of the American Statistical Association, 102*(479), 813–823.

Guynn, J. (2015, March 4). Meet the woman who coined #Black Lives Matter. *USA Today*. Retrieved from http://www.usatoday.com/story/tech/2015/03/04/alicia-garza-black-lives-matter/24341593/

hooks, b. (2003). *Teaching community: A pedagogy of hope*. New York, NY: Routledge.

Independent Sector. (2016, May 31). The value of volunteer time [Factsheet]. Retrieved from https://www.independentsector.org/resource/the-value-of-volunteer-time/

Innis, M. (2016, June 14). Australian mammal is first made extinct by human-driven climate change, scientists say. *New York Times*. Retrieved from http://www.nytimes.com/2016/06/15/world/australia/climate-change-bramble-cay-rodent.html

International Union for Conservation of Nature. (2017).

Jervis, R. (2014). Mental disorders keep thousands of homeless on streets. *USA Today*. Retrieved from http://www.usatoday.com/story/news/nation/2014/08/27/mental-health-homeless-series/14255283/

Kahne, J., & Westheimer, J. (1999). In the service of what? The politics of service learning. In J. Claus & C. Ogden (Eds.), *Service learning for youth empowerment and social change* (pp. 25–42). New York, NY: Peter Lang.

Kilgo, C. A., Ezell Sheets, J. K., & Pascarella, E. T. (2015). The link between high-impact practices and student learning: Some longitudinal evidence. *Higher Education, 69*(4), 509–525.

Kohl, H. R. (2005). *She would not be moved: How we tell the story of Rosa Parks and the Montgomery bus boycott.* New York, NY: The New Press.

Kozol, J. (1991). *Savage inequalities: Children in America's schools.* New York, NY: Crown.

Kretzmann, J. P., & McKnight, J. (1993). *Building communities from the inside out.* Evanston, IL: Center for Urban Affairs and Policy Research, Neighborhood Innovations Network.

Langer, E. (2014, March). Mindfulness in the age of complexity. *Harvard Business Review.* Retrieved from https://hbr.org/2014/03/mindfulness-in-the-age-of-complexity

Matson, J. (2013, May 1). Women are earning greater share of STEM degrees, but doctorates remain gender-skewed. *Scientific American.* Retrieved from http://www.scientificamerican.com/article/women-earning-greater-share-stem-degrees-doctorates-remain-gender-skewed/

McIntosh, P. (1988). *White privilege: Unpacking the invisible knapsack.* Retrieved from https://nationalseedproject.org/white-privilege-unpacking-the-invisible-knapsack

Merriam-Webster. (2017). Empathy [Def. 1]. Retrieved from http://www.merriam-webster.com/dictionary/empathy

Mezirow, J. (1997). Transformative learning: Theory to practice. *New Directions for Adult and Continuing Education, 1997*(74), 5–6.

Mitchell, T. D. (2008). Traditional vs. critical service-learning: Engaging the literature to differentiate two models. *Michigan Journal of Community Service Learning, 14*(2), 50–65.

National Center for Education Statistics. (n.d.). *Fast facts.* Retrieved from https://nces.ed.gov/fastfacts/display.asp?id=72

National Task Force on Civic Learning and Democratic Engagement. (2012). *A crucible moment: College learning and democracy's future.* Washington DC: American Association of Colleges and Universities.

Orfield, M. (2002). *American metro politics: The new suburban reality.* Washington DC: Brookings Institution Press.

Palmer, P. (1987). Community, conflict, and ways of knowing: Ways to deepen our educational agenda. *Change, 19*(5), 20–25.

Ruark, J. (2010, January 3). The Chronicle review: The art of living mindfully. *The Chronicle of Higher Education.* Retrieved from https://www.chronicle.com/article/The-Art-of-Living-Mindfully/63292

Sandy, M. (2007). *Community voices: A California campus compact study on partnerships.* Retrieved from http://www.cacampuscompact.org/pdf/CACC_CommunityVoices_FinalReport.pdf

Schön, D. A. (1983). *The reflective practitioner: How professionals think in action.* New York, NY: Basic Books.

Schussler, D. L. (2006). Defining dispositions: Wading through murky waters. *The Teacher Educator, 41*(4), 251–268.

Stanfield, R. B. (Ed.). (2000). *The art of focused conversation: 100 ways to access group wisdom in the workplace.* Gabriola, BC: New Society.

Stoecker, R. (2016). *Liberating service learning and the rest of higher education civic engagement.* Philadelphia, PA: Temple University Press.

Stoecker, R., & Tryon, E. A. (Eds.). (2009). *The unheard voices: Community organizations and service learning.* Philadelphia, PA: Temple University Press.

Strain, C. R. (2006). Moving like a starfish: Beyond a unilinear model of student transformation in service learning classes. *Journal of College and Character, 8*(1), 1.

Tajfel, H. (Ed.). (2010). *Social identity and intergroup relations.* Cambridge, UK: Cambridge University Press.

Tervalon, M., & Murray-Garcia, J. (1998). Cultural humility versus cultural competence: A critical distinction in defining physician training outcomes in multicultural education. *Journal of Health Care for the Poor and Underserved, 9*(2), 117–125.

Tuck, E. (2009). Suspending damage: A letter to communities. *Harvard Educational Review, 79*(3), 409–428.

Urban, M. C. (2015). Accelerating extinction risk from climate change. *Science, 348*(6234), 571–573.

U.S. Department of Agriculture Economic Research Service. (2017). *Definitions of food security.* Retrieved from http://www.ers.usda.gov/topics/food-nutrition-assistance/food-security-in-the-us/definitions-of-food-security.aspx

U.S. Department of Housing and Urban Development. (2016). *The 2016 annual homeless assessment report to Congress.* Retrieved from https://www.hudexchange.info/resources/documents/2016-AHAR-Part-1.pdf

Vargas, J. A. (2011, June 22). My life as an undocumented immigrant. *New York Times Magazine.* Retrieved from http://www.nytimes.com/2011/06/26/magazine/my-life-as-an-undocumented-immigrant.html

Watanabe, T., & Newell, S. (2016, July 13). Four in 10 UC students do not have a consistent source of high-quality, nutritious food, survey says. *Los Angeles Times.* Retrieved from http://www.latimes.com/local/california/la-me-uc-food-insecurity-07112016-snap-story.html

Wilson, W. (1902). Princeton for the nation's service: The inaugural address of President Woodrow Wilson. *Princeton Alumni Weekly, 3*(6), 89–98.

World Wildlife Fund. (2016). *Living planet report 2016: Risk and resilience in a new era.* Gland, Switzerland.

Yosso, T. J. (2005). Whose culture has capital? A critical race theory discussion of community cultural wealth. *Race, Ethnicity and Education, 8*(1), 69–91.

Zarya, V. (2016). The percentage of female CEOs in the Fortune 500 drops to 4%. *Fortune.* Retrieved from http://fortune.com/2016/06/06/women-ceos-fortune-500-2016/

ABOUT THE AUTHORS

David M. Donahue is director of the Leo T. McCarthy Center for Public Service and the Common Good and professor of education at the University of San Francisco (USF). Before coming to USF in 2015, he was the interim provost and associate provost at Mills College in Oakland, California, and worked there for more than 20 years as a professor of education, where he taught and advised doctoral students, teacher credential candidates, and undergraduates. He has a PhD in education from Stanford University and a BA in history from Brown University. His research interests include teacher learning generally and learning from service-learning and the arts specifically. He has also published on LGBTQ issues in education. He is coeditor of *Democratic Dilemmas of Teaching Service Learning: Curricular Strategies for Success* (Stylus, 2011); *Art-Centered Learning Across the Curriculum: Integrating Contemporary Art in the Secondary School Classroom* (Teachers College Press, 2014); and *Artful Teaching: Integrating the Arts for Understanding Across the Curriculum* (Teachers College Press, 2010).

Star Plaxton-Moore is director of community-engaged learning at the Leo T. McCarthy Center for Public Service and the Common Good at the University of San Francisco (USF). She directs institutional support for community-engaged courses and oversees public service programs for undergraduates, including the Public Service and Community Engagement Minor. She designed and implements an annual Community-Engaged Learning and Teaching Fellowship program for USF faculty and other professional development offerings that bring together faculty and community partners as colearners. Her scholarship focuses on faculty development for community-engaged teaching and scholarship, student preparation, assessment of civic learning outcomes, and community engagement in institutional culture and practice. Plaxton-Moore holds an MEd from George Washington University and is currently completing course work for an EdD in international and multicultural education at USF. In addition to being a committed community engagement scholar and professional, Plaxton-Moore loves spending time with her two curious and affectionate children and spouse.

INDEX